CMMI® SCAMPI℠ Distilled

CMMI® SCAMPI℠ Distilled

Appraisals for Process Improvement

Dennis M. Ahern
Jim Armstrong
Aaron Clouse
Jack R. Ferguson
Will Hayes
Kenneth E. Nidiffer

▲▼ Addison-Wesley

Upper Saddle River, NJ • Boston • Indianapolis • San Francisco
New York • Toronto • Montreal • London • Munich • Paris
Madrid • Capetown • Sydney • Tokyo • Singapore • Mexico City

Carnegie Mellon
Software Engineering Institute

The SEI Series in Software Engineering

The publisher offers excellent discounts on this book when ordered in quantity for bulk purchases or special sales, which may include electronic versions and/or custom covers and content particular to your business, training goals, marketing focus, and branding interests. For more information, please contact:

> U.S. Corporate and Government Sales
> (800) 382-3419
> corpsales@pearsontechgroup.com

For sales outside of the U.S., please contact:

> International Sales
> international@pearsoned.com

Visit us on the Web: www.awprofessional.com

Library of Congress Catalog Number: 2004115900

ISBN: 0-32-122876-6
Text printed in the United States on recycled paper at R. R. Donnelley in Crawfordsville, Indiana.
First printing, March 2005

Contents

Figure List

Preface

Capability Maturity Model Integration (CMMI) is a new way of approaching integrated, model-based process improvement for engineering development.[1] This book describes an appraisal method that is a part of the CMMI Product Suite. The method is called the *Standard CMMI Appraisal Method for Process Improvement*, or SCAMPI. (The team was really cookin' when it came up with this acronym!) To use SCAMPI to perform an appraisal on your organization is a significant effort that can require a major investment of resources. This book will help you to better understand what SCAMPI is, and how you can make your investment in process improvement pay off.

One primary reason for you to select a model (such as CMMI) as a tool to improve the quality of your organization's processes and products is that the model contains established "best practices," which can comprise a consistent long-term focus for process improvement planning. In addition to these best practices, the model provides a framework by which your processes may be improved in defined increments, so that their capability to produce planned results is increased. You can use a SCAMPI appraisal not only to identify process improvement opportunities, but also to measure your progress and establish a benchmark (against the CMMI model) that characterizes how far your organization is along the road to increased process capability. These results can be used to chart improvements over time, or to make comparisons among different parts of your organization or across different organizations.[2]

---

[1] Two books are available that present the CMMI models, and they are recommended as good sources for an understanding of what CMMI is all about. *CMMI Distilled, Second Edition* (Ahern, D., Clouse, A., and Turner, R., Boston: Addison-Wesley, 2004) concisely describes the models and other parts of the CMMI Product Suite, while also providing practical guidance on the use of those materials. *CMMI: Guidelines for Process Integration and Product Improvement* (Chrissis, M.B., Konrad, M., and Shrum, S., Boston: Addison-Wesley, 2003) introduces the CMMI models, presents a detailed case study of their use, and explains the entire CMMI model (filling most of the book), with all the model variants merged together into a single presentation.

[2] Opinions may vary on the value of, or the degree of objectivity in, comparisons across organizations based on SCAMPI appraisals. In this book we will explore reasons for the various opinions on this topic. Clearly, when an acquirer uses a measure of process capability as part of the basis for selecting a supplier and a supplier organization prospers or fails based on such choices, there is a lot of interest in making SCAMPI appraisals sufficiently objective.

Purpose

This book has a fourfold purpose. First, we wish to explore and clarify model-based process improvement and how it compares and relates to other current approaches to increasing your organization's process capability and performance. As you invest resources in process improvement, how much of that investment should be in CMMI and conducting SCAMPI appraisals? Second, we will present salient aspects of the new SCAMPI method. This information is essential to making a SCAMPI appraisal benefit your organization. Third, we will compare and contrast the "internal" use of SCAMPI as a process improvement tool to the "external" use of SCAMPI as a tool for evaluating potential suppliers, or monitoring existing suppliers. Finally, we wish to explore strategic decisions for using SCAMPI appraisals in different kinds of organizations.

Audience

The primary intended audience for this book is any member of an engineering development organization who has a role in promoting internal process improvement or in appraising the process capability of suppliers.[3] Whether you chose this role or someone chose it for you (such things happen, occasionally), you should be able use this book to understand and make good decisions about CMMI SCAMPI appraisals. Our audience includes executives, middle managers, team leaders, acquisition specialists, quality specialists, marketing personnel, process improvement champions, and the often overlooked and overworked process improvement practitioners.

Executives who sponsor a SCAMPI appraisal will find guidance on the key decisions that they will confront during the planning for and execution of an appraisal, and will gain a better understanding of the benefits that they can expect. Middle managers, and team leaders, as well as program or project managers will find information about their roles during the conduct of an appraisal. Their key role is to supply information to the appraisal team on the processes actually followed by the organization. Those with an acquirer role will learn about the

---

[3] Many of the same principles and techniques for process improvement that apply in engineering development organizations can apply more broadly in other kinds of organizations. CMMI was sponsored and developed with an eye to its application in engineering development, but much of it may find useful application in a broader context.

value and limitations of using SCAMPI appraisal results in supplier selection and monitoring. Of course, quality specialists have a central role in any process improvement effort or any appraisal of such an effort, and they will learn again why their role is so important. Did we say marketing personnel? You bet! Because acquirers may want to know about the CMMI rating of a potential supplier, those in marketing will gain an understanding of what such ratings mean and the value for their customers in being an organization with established, capable processes.

Process improvement champions need to build and maintain support for ongoing improvement activities, and when the time comes for an appraisal, they will be getting questions from all sides:

- How much did you say this is going to cost?
- You need us to provide evidence of *what?*
- Is this really going to help us?
- Why do we need to change this procedure when it's worked for us up until now?

And so on, and so on.

Most of what we present in this book will help process improvement champions deal with such questions and the stressful environment in which they are asked (but they are on their own in finding a good therapist). Those who implement process improvement have many roles to play in a SCAMPI appraisal, including gathering the objective evidence that an appraisal team needs to do its work and being interviewed during the appraisal. We will provide sufficient information to perform such roles well.

Speaking of appraisal teams, both SCAMPI lead appraisers and SCAMPI appraisal team members are an important part of our intended audience. They have the task of appraising organizational compliance against the CMMI model and assuring that the appraisal method is properly followed. As team members, they may or may not be part of the organization that is undergoing the appraisal. An organization may want an SEI-qualified lead appraiser from outside the organization in order to increase the perception that the results are reliable and sufficiently objective. A division of a large corporation may wish to bring in some team members from other locations, divisions, or sectors to introduce multiple perspectives. Whatever its makeup, the appraisal team has a key role in promoting process improvement across the organization. The information in this book can serve as a useful supplement to the training that those on the appraisal team receive.

Often, we suppose, you may have picked up this book because you have just been told that you are about to be interviewed by an appraisal team as part of a SCAMPI appraisal, and you aren't really sure what it is about or how to prepare. Don't panic! Read on!

Organization

This book is divided into three major parts.

Part I, "Why SCAMPI Now?" provides a summary of the CMMI Product Suite today, including the project, models, appraisal methods, and training. Part I also sets the stage by reviewing process appraisal strategies in the context of a process improvement model, as well as related techniques, quality initiatives, international standards, and other approaches that may affect how you address process improvement in your organization. It explores the question of whether an appraisal you conduct using an integrated model (like CMMI) must mandate that there are integrated processes in the organization.

Part II, "SCAMPI Appraisals," describes SCAMPI appraisals in detail. First, distinctive new aspects of the SCAMPI method are presented as a way of orienting readers who may be familiar with prior appraisal techniques, which are described briefly. Then an overview of SCAMPI includes its basic features, its modes of use (process improvement, supplier selection, and process monitoring), the sources for objective evidence that the appraisal team reviews, and indicators that the CMMI model practices have been implemented in the organization. The appraisal itself has three parts, including

- Preparation with the appraisal sponsor on objectives, plans, scope, team training, and data gathering
- On-site activities that start with reviewing data and conducting interviews, which is followed by generating preliminary observations, findings, and (possibly) ratings
- Production and report on the final appraisal results and subsequent follow-on activities

The SCAMPI method family consists of SCAMPI A, which is a "class A" (most rigorous) appraisal, and the less rigorous and less costly SCAMPI B and SCAMPI C methods that you can use either for their intrinsic benefits or as you lay the groundwork for a SCAMPI A appraisal.

Part II concludes by reviewing and contrasting SCAMPI as an appraisal tool for internal process improvement with SCAMPI as an appraisal tool used by an external entity, such as a customer. While SCAMPI is an integrated method that supports both uses, we explore how those uses may vary depending on its mode of use.

Having laid the foundation with a full presentation of SCAMPI, Part III, "Using SCAMPI," concludes with the discussion of various issues having to do with appraisals and process improvement. How can appraisals benefit an organization just starting process improvement, as opposed to a (so-called) high-maturity organization? How are appraisals best conducted across various disciplines, such as software and systems engineering? How does an organization comply with a CMMI model, conduct a successful SCAMPI appraisal, and at the same time meet the requirements of other standards and quality initiatives and respond adequately to customer-driven needs?

Two appendices are provided. The first is a glossary that defines special terms used by CMMI and SCAMPI and the second describes sample artifacts that an organization might use to show compliance with the CMMI practices.

The CMMI project is an ongoing effort, so something as time-restricted as a book must be adjusted as time passes and things change. We strived to provide you with information that is both timely and of lasting value, but it is important for you to have access to the latest information. To this end, the publisher has agreed to support this volume with updates through its Web site (www.awprofessional.com) and with further editions as appropriate.

Acknowledgments

The authors would like to acknowledge the efforts of those who were members of the CMMI Team, including those who participated on the Product Development Team and Steering Group, and especially those who participated on the Assessment Method Team, and then later the Appraisal Method Integrated Team. It was through the efforts of these latter groups that the *Appraisal Requirements for CMMI* (ARC) and SCAMPI were generated. The members of these teams may not agree with everything that we say here, but the book would not exist without their devoted and amazingly productive efforts over several years on behalf of CMMI.

Peter Gordon and other Addison-Wesley personnel were invaluable in helping us blend the significantly different writing styles of the six authors into coherent, readable prose. The reviewers engaged by the publisher, including several from the Software Engineering Institute, provided us with many useful improvement suggestions. Additionally, we would like to thank Dr. Rich Turner for his assistance in identifying the pictures that we used in the book, and Ralph Williams for providing example charts used in verifying generic practices.

Finally the authors would like to thank our families (and especially Pam, Carolyn, Debbi, Chris, Mary, and Karen) who provided support so that we could meet our production schedule. We love you.

Dennis, Jim, Aaron, Jack, Ken, and Will

Baltimore, Herndon, Dallas, Colorado Springs, Herndon, and Pittsburgh, February 2005

About the Authors

Dennis M. Ahern is an advisory engineer and manager for process improvement and industry initiatives at Northrop Grumman Corporation. Previously he taught at Yale University and the University of Maryland. He was the Deputy Project Manager of the CMMI Product Development Team and a coleader of the CMMI Editor Team. He was also a member of the CMMI Assessment Methodology Team and is an author of CMMI. He is coauthor of *CMMI Distilled, Second Edition* (Addison-Wesley, 2004). Dr. Ahern received his Ph.D. from the University of California, Irvine.

Jim Armstrong is Chief Technologist for Systems for the Systems and Software Consortium, Inc. (SSCI). He has 37 years of experience in systems development and is an assessor for systems engineering and CMMI appraisals. He was a member of the author teams for IEEE 1220, EIA/IS 731, CMMI, and SCAMPI among other standards. Jim has worked with companies of diverse size and products in implementing process improvement, application of CMMI, and preparation for SCAMPI appraisals.

Aaron Clouse is an Engineering Fellow at Raytheon Company. He has 30 years of experience in electronics systems and software engineering. He is a member of the CMMI Model Team, is an authorized Introduction to CMMI instructor, and has participated in several appraisals. He coauthored both CMMI itself and *CMMI Distilled, Second Edition*.

Jack R. Ferguson is Manager of the SEI Appraisal Program. He has 39 years of experience in engineering, mainly related to the U.S. space program, and received the U.S. Air Force Research and Development Award for his work on Global Positioning System spacecraft attitude control. Dr. Ferguson also led the teams that developed the Software Acquisition CMM and the initial CMMI Product Suite, and recently spent two years in the Office of the Secretary of Defense as Director of Software Intensive Systems. He has a Ph.D. from the University of Texas at Austin.

Will Hayes is Senior Member of the Technical Staff of the Software Engineering Institute. He has been with the Software Engineering Institute (SEI) for 15 years, where he has held a number of positions focused on measurement, process improvement, and process appraisals. He is currently serving as the Quality Manager for the SEI Appraisal Program, a position he helped define. Will has extensive experience in process improvement consulting, process appraisals, and professional training. He has trained hundreds of lead appraisers and process improvement professionals, supporting the creation and/or delivery of courses focused on maturity models, measurement, statistical process control, and process appraisals. Will was a member of the Appraisal Method Integrated Team, which developed the SCAMPI V1.1 method, where he served as the primary author of the Method Definition Document.

Kenneth E. Nidiffer is Vice President of SSCI, with more than 43 years of experience in the marketing, research, development, maintenance, and acquisition of software-intensive systems. He has held several executive-level positions in the Department of Defense and the industry (e.g. Systems and Software Consortium, Inc., Northrop Grumman Corporation, and Fidelity Investments) where he has sponsored systematic process improvement initiatives. Dr. Nidiffer is currently responsible for program management and customer support activities that are responsive to the Consortium's 95-member company needs.

Part I

Why SCAMPI Now?

Deciding what dishes to prepare when planning a meal and knowing what complements what, which ingredients are in season and available, the taste preferences of the guests, and so on requires careful planning and a clear understanding of the range of options. Similarly, when working to improve processes in an enterprise, many tools and techniques are available. If CMMI is one of your "main courses" for process improvement, you should review other approaches and decide on the best mix of improvement techniques to ensure that all your stakeholders will enjoy the fruits of your work.

Part I Contents

Chapter 1. Process Appraisal Strategies

The reader is introduced to the CMMI Project and its products, together with comparisons between CMMI and other contemporary process improvement methods and tools.

Chapter 1

Process Appraisal Strategies

scam·pi (1) shrimp; (2) a dish (especially with shrimp) prepared
with a garlic-flavored butter sauce;[1] (3) a standard CMMI
appraisal method for process improvement

At work you might hear a lively debate around the coffee maker or before a meeting commences regarding the value of process to your organization. For some, focusing on process is the cornerstone of making an operation successful, allowing it to benefit from standard approaches that work well and to improve approaches that do not. For others, process is viewed at some distance and with suspicion; it signifies spending too much time on non-value-added activity, focusing on form rather than substance, and on documentation rather than individual creativity and initiative.

This dichotomy for or against process plays itself out in organizational management philosophies. At the first meeting of employees with a new upper-management team, you might hear: "I will be exploring concerns I have heard expressed that perhaps we have gone too far with process." Do not be overly concerned. For those who believe strongly in the importance of process, including the authors of this book, a sound approach to process improvement entails working with upper management to move beyond these opposing positions and

---

[1] We provide a recipe for shrimp scampi toward the end of the book, prior to Appendix A.

encompass both perspectives. We should be advocates for standard organizational processes as well as advocates for individual initiative, and never demean or underestimate the critical importance of personnel resources to running a successful operation. We should always seek to remove non-value-added steps in processes, which may inhibit the achievement of business objectives. We should seek to improve the efficiency and effectiveness of processes in order to free individuals and teams to use their abilities and to have time for creativity. We should not follow processes just for their own sake, but instead put in place processes that work to support the business, encouraging employees to do their best always.

One key tool to achieving such ends is the process appraisal. Historically, appraisals have had external uses (such as selecting or monitoring a supplier) in addition to their use for internal process improvement.[2] For each use, whether internal or external, the appraisal constitutes an intervention in the organization that is being appraised. The expenditure of resources to carry out such an intervention must ultimately be justified by the value that is returned. We will explore this topic as we discuss CMMI SCAMPI appraisals and as we compare them to other appraisal and improvement techniques that may be in use within an enterprise.

In this chapter, we will start by providing an overview of the CMMI project and the products that comprise the CMMI Product Suite. Then we review a range of process improvement techniques that in recent years have developed a following; their popularity is based on the belief that in different ways they add value. We will explore the difference between "model-based" process improvement efforts (such as CMMI) and other approaches that are not based on a model. It can be a challenge to figure out how, for example, CMMI, Lean, Six Sigma, and ISO 9000 are the same, how they are different, what value each brings

---

[2] Those who are looking into CMMI SCAMPI appraisals and who have some acquaintance with ISO/IEC 15504 (the recently revised international standard for process assessment) will be aware of a difference in terminology. For 15504, the most general term for a review of process is "assessment," and a process assessment may be either internal on one's own organization or external on another organization. In contrast for SCAMPI, the most general term for a review of process is "appraisal." The term "appraisal" replaces the terms that previously were used with the CMM for Software: for internal use ("assessment"), and for external use ("evaluation"). Hopefully, over time, the CMMI and ISO groups will collaborate and work toward uniform terminology.

to the table, and how their use may affect your appraisals. We want to help get you started on a path that makes sense for your entire enterprise. Also, we will explore the role of appraisals in any process improvement strategy.

1.1 Process Improvement Models and CMMI

Prior to the advent of CMMI, the most widely used process improvement model targeted software development: the *Capability Maturity Model for Software* (SW-CMM).[3] In the area of systems engineering, the *Systems Engineering Capability Model* (SECM)—EIA 731—was gaining converts.[4] Both the SW-CMM and EIA 731 were sources for CMMI, and each had an appraisal method associated with it (see Figure 1-1). The

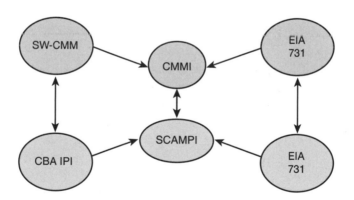

Figure 1-1: *Model and Appraisal Method Relationships*

---

[3] Paulk, Mark C., et al. *Capability Maturity Model for Software, Version 1.1 (CMU/SEI-93-TR-24; also ESC-TR-93-177).* Pittsburgh: Software Engineering Institute, Carnegie Mellon University, February 1993. Paulk, Mark C. et al. *The Capability Maturity Model: Guidelines for Improving the Software Process*, Reading, MA: Addison-Wesley, 1995.

[4] *EIA Standard, Systems Engineering Capability-EIA 731* (Part 1: Model, EIA 731-1, version 1.0; Part 2: Appraisal Method, EIA 732-2, version 1.0), 2002.

appraisal method for the SW-CMM was known as the *CMM-Based Appraisal for Internal Process Improvement* (CBA IPI),[5] while the appraisal method for EIA 731 was known as the *SECM Appraisal Method.* A central feature of the SW-CMM, EIA 731, CMMI, and similar models is their specification of "levels" to measure process capability and organizational maturity. As an organization makes use of such a model as a basis for appraising and improving its processes, it may find value in the "level" ratings both to measure its current status and to plan for future improvements.

When an appraisal is conducted by using any process improvement model (such as CMMI, CMM for Software, or SECM), the objectives are to identify process strengths and weaknesses, and (if desired) to provide "level" ratings for the organization. An appraisal team reviews the current practices within an organization and makes judgments about how well those practices comply with the requirements of the team's process improvement model. Those who create process improvement models must strive to include established best practices so that when an organization works to satisfy the model, it creates the solid foundation it needs for its process improvement efforts.

By deciding to use a particular process improvement model, an organization is implicitly endorsing the work of the team that created the model. After all, an organization could just start from scratch and work on its own to identify the best practices for its unique business environment. In doing this it would not rely on a model to establish requirements for its processes, but it would create its own process requirements. In some business environments this might be a wise course of action, but it would require a lot of confidence and insight. In contrast, there are benefits from adopting a standard set of process requirements, if indeed the model being considered has been constructed based on good empirical evidence of which processes are (typically) critical to the organization. Then if there are additional areas that are not covered in the model but are known to be important, the process improvement efforts can be expanded beyond the basic model requirements.

---

[5] Dunaway, D., and S. Masters, *CMM-Based Appraisal for Internal Process Improvement (CBA IPI): Method Description (CMU/SEI-96-TR-007).* Pittsburgh, Software Engineering Institute, Carnegie Mellon University, April 1996.

To better understand why an organization might want to choose a model to do process improvement, besides customer pressure, let us review both CMMI and several other approaches to process improvement that currently are attracting attention.

1.2 The CMMI Product Suite Today—V1.1

The CMMI Project was established to produce an integrated set of models, appraisal methods, and training for use across multiple disciplines, including systems and software engineering. First we will describe briefly how the CMMI Project is organized today, and then outline the primary products that comprise the CMMI Product Suite.

1.2.1 The CMMI Project

The Capability Maturity Model for Software has been used since the late 1980s to help organizations improve their software development processes. Its success could be measured in how many other models were created inspired by the CMM for Software, which resulted in various discipline-unique models. However, model variations cause conflicts for an organization when multiple models are used; for example, one model for software and a different one for systems engineering. The U.S. Department of Defense (DOD) and the National Defense Industrial Association (NDIA) sponsored the CMMI Project. The objective was to integrate three key closely related models into a single framework that could be used for systems engineering, software, and integrated product development.[6] This project was the Capability Maturity Model Integration (CMMI) Project.[7]

---

[6] The third source model was the *Integrated Product Development CMM*, version 0.98, which had been published in draft form only. Its development was halted by the onset of the CMMI effort.

[7] Members of the CMMI team were recruited from the DOD and industry. The following organizations supplied members to the CMMI Product Development Team: ADP Inc., AT&T Labs, BAE Systems, Boeing, Comarco Systems, Computer Sciences Corporation, Defense Logistics Agency, EER Systems, Ericsson Canada, Ernst and Young, General Dynamics, Harris Corporation, Honeywell, IBM, Integrated Systems Diagnostics, KPMG Consulting, Litton PRC, Lockheed Martin, MitoKen Solutions, Motorola, Northrop Grumman, Pacific Bell, Q-Labs, Raytheon, Rockwell Collins, Software Engineering Institute, Software Productivity Consortium, Sverdrup Corporation, TeraQuest, THALES, TRW, U.S. Air Force, U.S. Army, U.S. Federal Aviation Administration, U.S. Institute for Defense Analyses, U.S. National Reconnaissance Office, U.S. National Security Agency, and U.S. Navy.

CMMI Milestones	
1997	CMMI initiated by U.S. Department of Defense and NDIA
1998	First team meeting held
1999	Concept of operations released First pilot completed
2000	Additional pilots completed CMMI-SE/SW and CMMI-SE/SW/IPPD version 1.0 released for initial use CMMI-SE/SW/IPPD/SS version 1.0 released for piloting SCAMPI V1.0 Method Definition Document released Appraisal Requirements for CMMI (ARC) V1.0 released
2001	SCAMPI V1.1 Method Definition Document released Appraisal Requirements for CMMI (ARC) V1.1 released
2002	CMMI-SE/SW, CMMI-SE/SW/IPPD, CMMI-SE/SW/IPPD/SS, and CMMI-SW version 1.1 released SCAMPI V1.1 Method Implementation Guidance for Government Source Selection and Contract Process Monitoring released
2003-2006	Focus on transition into use

The project was organized into teams that supported the development of the components within the CMMI Framework. The teams addressed the models, appraisals, and training. We will explore each of these framework elements. Today, the CMMI Product Team is organized as shown in Figure 1-2.

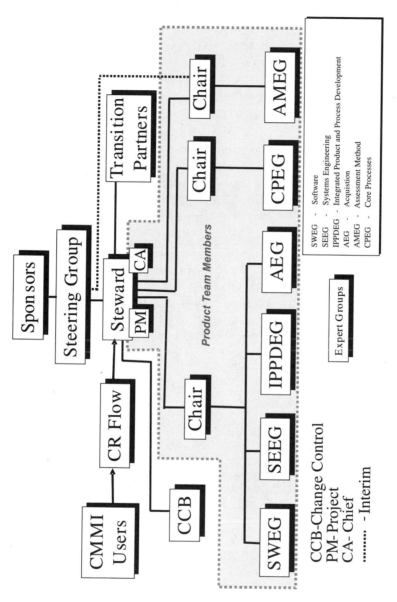

Figure 1-2: *CMMI Project Organization Chart*

The DOD and NDIA are still the sponsors of the CMMI Project. The Steering Group members represent industry, DOD, and the Steward. The Steward responsibility was assigned to the Software Engineering Institute of Carnegie Mellon University. The Steward provides training for instructors and lead appraisers, maintains the CMMI Framework, and supports the deployment of CMMI by managing a partner program. Partners are licensed by the Steward to provide appraisal and training services. In addition, the Steward supports the configuration control board whose members represent the key stakeholders, and it provides the *Program Manager* (PM) and the *Chief Architect* (CA) for the Framework. Expert Groups are used to work on improvements to the CMMI Framework, as shown in Figure 1-2.

1.2.2 The CMMI Models

Integrating the three source models was a significant challenge for the CMMI Team. For detailed information about the integrated model that resulted from the effort, refer to two excellent sources: *CMMI: Guidelines for Process Integration and Product Improvement*[8] and *CMMI Distilled*.[9] What appeared to be a simple merge of three source models turned out to have many issues, including

- *Process area* (PA) partitioning (number of PAs)
- Staged or continuous representation
- Number of practices
- Use of advanced practices
- Overall size of the model
- Clarity of practices and ability to appraise them
- Include Generic Attributes or not

In fact, the first version of the CMMI model released for review (V0.2) was considerably larger than subsequent versions 1.0 and 1.1. The level of detail at the practice level in V0.2, an amalgam of the details from the three source models, made the integrated model so large that any

---

[8] *CMMI: Guidelines for Process Integration and Product Improvement* (Chrissis, M.B., Konrad, M., and Shrum, S., Reading, MA: Addison-Wesley, 2003) introduces the CMMI models, presents a detailed case study of their use, and explains the entire CMMI model (filling most of the book), with all the model variants merged together into a single presentation.

[9] *CMMI Distilled* (Ahern, D., Clouse, A., and Turner, R., Reading, MA: Addison-Wesley, Second Edition, 2003) concisely describes the models and other parts of the CMMI Product Suite, together with practical guidance on the use of these materials.

expectation of a reasonable appraisal was deemed impossible to achieve. Each CMMI review and release cycle reduced the number of practices and number of process areas, in many cases by combining or generalizing them. Even with this reduction in model size, the current CMMI model is still quite robust. An appraisal challenge still exists in that the amount of time and effort required to conduct a CMMI SCAMPI appraisal represents a significant organizational investment.

The CMMI Framework allows several different models to be generated for different kinds of organizations. Currently, the following models are supported in both staged and continuous representations:[10]

- CMMI-SE/SW/IPPD/SS
- CMMI-SE/SW/IPPD
- CMMI-SE/SW
- CMMI-SW

In general, the only difference among these models is the process area content and amplifications.[11] For example, the only difference between the CMMI-SW and CMMI-SE/SW is that the amplifications for systems engineering contained in CMMI-SE/SW are not in the CMMI-SW model; all other components are exactly the same. A SCAMPI appraisal may be conducted using any current version of the CMMI model.

Figure 1-3 shows the structure of the CMMI staged representation. The process areas in the staged representation are organized by maturity level; each process area exists at one maturity level. The practices within each process area are structured by goals. The generic practices (GPs) are organized by common features similar to those found in the CMM for Software.

In the continuous representation, process areas are organized not by maturity levels but by process categories, as shown in Figure 1-4. Each process area spans all the levels in the model. The four process-area categories are Process Management, Project Management, Engineering, and Support. Notice that unlike the staged representation, the generic practices are not organized by the common features in the continuous

---

[10] SE = Systems Engineering; SW = Software; IPPD = Integrated Process and Product Development; SS = Supplier Sourcing.

[11] Amplifications contain discipline-specific information about how to apply the CMMI models to one specific discipline, such as software or systems engineering.

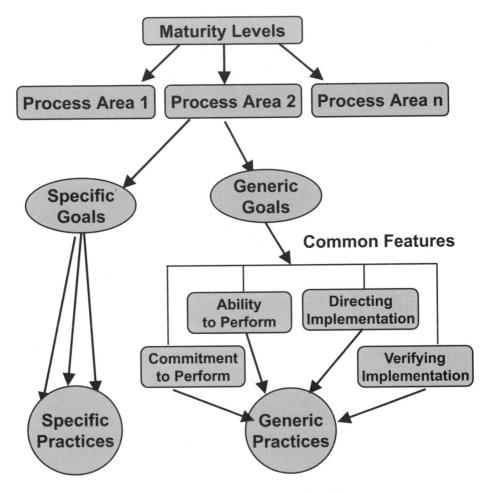

Figure 1-3: *Staged Representation Structure*

representation. Common features are used only as organization elements in the staged models; the generic practices are essentially the same in both representations, staged and continuous.

There are 25 process areas in the entire CMMI (V1.1) Framework. Table 1-1 shows a summary of those process areas, and for each one a count of some of the key elements (such as goals and practices) that are important during an appraisal.

The goals and practices are critical to the appraisal. Subpractices comprise informative material that can be used to understand the meaning of the practices. The large number in the right column shows why it

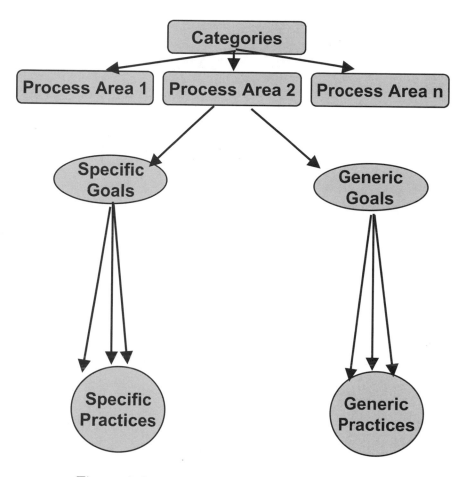

Figure 1-4: *Continuous Representation Structure*

would not be practical to expect evidence for every one of the subpractices during an appraisal.

Let's take a closer look at the CMMI appraisal methods.

1.2.3 The CMMI Appraisal Methods

The product development teams produced three key appraisal documents: the *Appraisal Requirements for CMMI (ARC),*[12] the *Standard CMMI Appraisal Method for Process Improvement* (SCAMPI) *Method*

---

[12] *Appraisal Requirements for CMMI, Version 1.1 (ARC, V1.1), (CMU/SEI-2001-TR-034)*. Pittsburgh, Software Engineering Institute, Carnegie Mellon University, December 2001.

Table 1-1: *CMMI Model Size Summary*

Process Area (PA)	PA Acronym	M L	Category	Goals	Practices	Number of Subpractices
Causal Analysis and Resolution	CAR	5	Support	2	5	13
Configuration Management	CM	2	Support	3	7	38
Decision Analysis and Resolution	DAR	3	Support	2	6	22
Integrated Project Management for IPPD	IPM	3	Project Mgmt	4	13	70
Integrated Supplier Management	ISM	3	Project Mgmt	2	5	18
Integrated Teaming	IT	3	Project Mgmt	2	8	29
Measurement and Analysis	MA	2	Support	2	8	34
Organizational Environment for Integration	OEI	3	Support	2	6	26
Organizational Innovation and Deployment	OID	5	Process Mgmt	2	7	47
Organizational Process Definition	OPD	3	Process Mgmt	1	5	34
Organizational Process Focus	OPF	3	Process Mgmt	2	7	42
Organizational Process Performance	OPP	4	Process Mgmt	1	5	20

Process Area	Abbrev		Category			
Organizational Training	OT	3	Process Mgmt	2	7	28
Product Integration	PI	3	Eng	2	4	22
Project Monitoring and Control	PMC	2	Project Mgmt	3	9	38
Project Planning	PP	2	Project Mgmt	2	10	37
Process and Product Quality Assurance	PPQA	2	Support	3	14	36
Quantitative Project Management	QPM	4	Project Mgmt	2	8	42
Requirements Development	RD	3	Eng	3	12	35
Requirements Management	REQM	2	Eng	1	5	18
Risk Management	RSKM	3	Project Mgmt	3	7	25
Supplier Agreement Management	SAM	2	Project Mgmt	2	7	37
Technical Solution	TS	3	Eng	3	11	52
Validation	VAL	3	Eng	2	5	19
Verification	VER	3	Eng	3	8	44
Totals				55	189	826

Definition Document (MDD),[13] and the SCAMPI Version 1.1: Method Implementation Guidance for Government Source Selection and Contract Process Monitoring.[14]

The ARC consists of a set of high-level design criteria for developing, defining, and using appraisal methods based on the CMMI models. The SCAMPI V1.1 Method Implementation Guidance for Government Source Selection and Contract Process Monitoring provides guidance to government personnel and their supporting organizations for fulfilling the objectives of the SCAMPI method in their acquisition environments. The SCAMPI Method Definition Document describes the requirements, activities, and practices associated with each of the processes that comprise the SCAMPI method. It is intended to be one of the infrastructure elements within which SCAMPI Lead Appraisers conduct a SCAMPI appraisal. Precise listings of required practices, parameters, and variation limits, as well as optional practices and guidance for enacting the method, are covered in this document.

We will present the appraisal method in detail in Chapter 3, "SCAMPI Class A Method Definition."

1.2.4 The CMMI Training

In addition to the model and appraisal teams, the product development team included a training team, responsible for developing training materials as a part of the CMMI Framework. Several versions of training materials were developed to support both the staged and continuous representations of the model, including the following courses:

- Introduction to CMMI
- Intermediate Concepts of CMMI
- Introduction to CMMI Instructor Training
- SCAMPI Lead Appraiser Training (SLAT)

The *Introduction to CMMI* course introduces participants to the CMMI Model and its fundamental concepts. This three-day course

---

[13] *Standard CMMI Appraisal Method for Process Improvement Version 1.1: Method Definition Document (CMU/SEI-2001-HB-001)*. Pittsburgh, Software Engineering Institute, Carnegie Mellon University, December 2001.

[14] Standard CMMI Appraisal Method for Process Improvement (SCAMPI), Version 1.1: Method Implementation Guidance for Government Source Selection and Contract Process Monitoring (CMU/SEI-2002-HB-002). Pittsburgh, Software Engineering Institute, Carnegie Mellon University, September 2002.

helps prepare participants to make valid judgments regarding an organization's implementation of the process areas. The course is helpful in identifying issues that should be addressed in performing process improvement as structured by the CMMI model. This course is required for SCAMPI appraisal team members, lead appraisers, and CMMI instructors.

The *Intermediate Concepts of CMMI* course provides participants with a deeper understanding of the CMMI models and their fundamental concepts. It emphasizes in greater detail the process areas, the relationships among process areas, as well as the relationships among other CMMI components. The course is presented in a facilitative style to encourage dialogue among participants and instructors. It helps prepare participants to make valid judgments regarding their organization's implementation of the process areas.

This is a five-day course composed of lectures and class exercises, with ample opportunity for participant demonstration, questions, and discussions. This course in intended for the following participants:

- Candidate lead appraisers and team leaders for the SCAMPI Appraisal Method
- Systems and software engineers, and process personnel who need a more in-depth knowledge of the CMMI models
- Candidate instructors interested in becoming authorized to teach the *Introduction to CMMI* course

The *Introduction to CMMI Instructor Training* course prepares participants to become authorized instructors for the *Introduction to CMMI* course. This three-day "train the trainer" course provides participants with the opportunity to prepare for and present CMMI concepts. The trainers in this course provide feedback to the candidate instructors, evaluating each candidate's presentations.

After being observed teaching a course by an SEI trainer and receiving a satisfactory recommendation, participants may then provide training services for their own organization or other organizations. (Note that training services are defined in an organization's partnership agreement with the SEI.)

The *SCAMPI Lead Appraiser Training* course prepares participants to become SCAMPI appraisal team leaders. It is for participants who have appraisal experience and wish to become authorized SCAMPI Lead Appraisers in the SEI Appraisal Program.

After successfully completing the course, being observed by an SEI-qualified observing lead appraiser, and receiving a satisfactory recommendation, participants may provide SCAMPI appraisal services for their own organization or other organizations. In addition, they may deliver appraisal training to appraisal teams, using SEI materials in accordance with their organization's partnership agreement with the SEI.

CMMI Instructor and SCAMPI Lead Appraiser Workshops provide annual upgrades to the training and appraisal methods.

Other training courses of various lengths and focus have been generated by some of the partners. Examples are one-day or two-day CMMI awareness courses and CDs with videotaped presentations of the CMMI materials. Other organizations have developed two-hour and four-hour presentations for managers. The NDIA and SEI co-sponsor the CMMI Technology Conference held in Denver each November to provide a forum for sharing and learning between all of the CMMI user community. Regional workshops are held quarterly, as well.

With this basic understanding of what constitutes the CMMI Product Suite today, we will now review other process improvement initiatives, starting with Lean.

1.3 Lean[15]

The Lean approach to process improvement is a result of the *Lean Aerospace Initiative* (LAI), a consortium of the U.S. Government, industry, labor, and universities.[16] In the early 1990s, the U.S. Air Force began to ask whether the advances that had been made in Lean

---

[15] Hal Wilson, the Northrop Grumman member of the CMMI Steering Group, developed a comparative white paper on CMMI and Lean. It was called "Position Paper on Government Use of Lean Enterprise Self-Assessment Tool (LESAT) for Benchmarking." His ideas in that paper helped inform our discussion in this section.

[16] There is information on the Web about Lean and the Lean Aerospace Initiative at http://lean.mit.edu/. Two important books on Lean are Womack, J.; D. Jones; and D. Roos; *The Machine that Changed the World: The Story of Lean Production* (Rawson Associates, New York, 1990); and Murman, E., et al., *Lean Enterprise Value: Insights from MIT's Lean Aerospace Initiative* (Palgrave, New York, 2002).

automobile production in Japan could be applied to the U.S. aerospace industry. As a result, LAI was begun at the *Massachusetts Institute of Technology* (MIT) in 1993. Lean was created to reduce the cost of producing aircraft and other aerospace products. In addition to affordability, a Lean approach is one that focuses on the elimination or reduction of waste to improve the flow of information and work products, and the efficient creation of value for the enterprise.

A Lean approach can be applied across an entire enterprise, including manufacturing, finance, and virtually any activity in which there could be inefficiency in how things are done. Outside of manufacturing, the Lean concepts can also be applied to most product development processes and might be used (in a modified form) in the delivery of services. The Lean Enterprise Model contains 12 overarching practices:

1. Identify and optimize enterprise flow
2. Implement integrated product and process development
3. Maintain challenge of existing processes
4. Ensure seamless information flow
5. Ensure process capability and maturation
6. Maximize stability in a changing environment
7. Optimize capability and utilization of people
8. Develop relationships based on mutual trust and commitment
9. Nurture a learning environment
10. Make decisions at lowest possible level
11. Promote Lean leadership at all levels
12. Continuously focus on the customer

A key activity in a Lean approach is to focus on the processes by which *value* is added to work products. Then, a mapping of the "value-stream" is created to determine when value is added to work products and when it is not. The central objective is to reduce the time during which no value is added, such as a part sitting unused for days in a queue.

Lean is intended for internal use within an enterprise, and (unlike CMMI and SCAMPI) its proponents pointedly and adamantly discourage its use for comparisons between organizations.[17] The *Lean Enterprise Self-Assessment Tool* (LESAT) has a broad focus on the product life cycle across the enterprise and takes into account many activities that are to some degree unique to individual companies. It is a self-assessment that determines the state of "Leanness" in an organization and its readiness for change. It uses a concept of five levels to rate each practice on a scale from least capable (level 1) to world class (level 5); see Table 1-2.

Table 1-2: *Lean Generic Level Definitions*

Level	Definition
Level 1	Some awareness of this practice; sporadic improvement activities may be underway in a few areas.
Level 2	General awareness; informal approach deployed in a few areas with varying degrees of effectiveness and sustainment.
Level 3	A systematic approach/methodology deployed in varying stages across most areas; facilitated with metrics; good sustainment.
Level 4	On-going refinement and continuous improvement across the enterprise; improvement gains are sustained.
Level 5	Exceptional, well-defined, innovative approach is fully deployed across the extended enterprise (across internal and external value streams); recognized as best practice.

---

[17] At some point, the proponents of CMMI may wish to re-examine the trade between the value of CMMI as a tool that purports to provide an objective basis of comparison across diverse organizations, and its value as a collection of best practices that can support internal process improvement. In fact it is unclear the extent to which these two objectives are compatible in the real world. In many organizations today that are suppliers to the DOD, because CMMI is seen as an auditing tool needed to qualify for doing business, management in those organizations (as opposed to the CMMI faithful) seldom think of CMMI as a tool for process improvement. The message that you must have been appraised at some level "x" to be successful, and the large cost involved in attaining a given maturity level can effectively mask any thought that CMMI could be useful for the day-to-day needs to improve processes. In this regard the contrast between Lean and CMMI deserves review.

Leadership and a strong infrastructure are regarded as keys in the progression of a practice to level 5 status.

Clearly, both CMMI and LAI have considerable value. First, we will describe the similarities of the two approaches and then the differences. The genesis of both the LESAT and CMMI SCAMPI is similar but the focus is different. To improve performance and efficiency, sections of the U.S. Government, industry and academia initiated both Lean and CMMI. While the initial focus in Lean was on manufacturing, the initial focus in CMMI is on systems and software engineering principles and practices. Both highlight the importance of an *integrated process and product development* (IPPD) approach.

The Lean Enterprise Model and the CMMI models both are extensible, as are their respective assessment methods (LESAT and SCAMPI). Both the CMMI and LAI ultimately focus on the enterprise. Many of the early Lean and CMMI initiatives focused on picking the "low hanging fruit." Viewed as a collection of practices with names such as "Kaizen," Lean can be implemented in production operations with little or no integration with other enterprise functions or processes. CMMI has a similar heritage in that its predecessors initially focused on those elements that were least integrated—a bottoms-up versus top-down approach. For example, the maturity level 2 practices focus on management activities that can be implemented at the project level (versus the organizational level). While some benefits were gained with these efforts, the results were often less beneficial than had been hoped. It is now recognized that the full benefits of Lean and CMMI can be realized only by rethinking the entire enterprise. As a result, the assessment approaches can be viewed as "living" entities in that they will change as both the Lean Enterprise Model and CMMI evolve.

A key issue with respect to both SCAMPI and LESAT prior to an appraisal or assessment is the definition of the boundaries of the enterprise to be assessed. The "enterprise" may be a division of a major corporation, a particular site, a business unit, or other appropriate entity. The distinguishing characteristic of an enterprise is that it should have profit-and-loss or other performance accountability. Another characteristic of an enterprise is that it usually includes the life-cycle core processes (such as program management, requirement definition, product development, supply chain, production, and support) and the enabling processes (such as finance, human resources, and information systems). The particular nature of the enterprise to be assessed will define at an enterprise level its senior leadership, customers, suppliers, and other stakeholders.

The "model" approach used by CMMI and LAI are similar and the assessment frameworks (SCAMPI and LESAT) assess compliance to their specific models. SCAMPI and LESAT assess several similar key practices. Given the similarities between the CMMI and LAI initiatives, a partial cross mapping of the Lean Aerospace Initiative enabling practices to CMMI is presented in Table 1-3.

The assessment approaches are similar. Like SCAMPI, the LESAT was designed to help an organization assess its progress in its transformation. It is expected that the assessment will be performed on a regular, periodic schedule. The outcomes of a particular assessment should provide guidance to the organization in refining and adjusting its continuous improvement plans. Several alternative approaches to performance assessment were examined and compared. The LAI approach that best satisfies the user requirements is called a Capability Maturity Matrix. There are two primary steps in developing a Capability Maturity Matrix. The first is to determine the particular factors against which the organization will be assessed. After the factors are specified, the progressive maturity levels related to each factor must be carefully constructed.

Resistance to Change with Lean and CMMI

Lean might be supported by Six Sigma and other process improvement mechanisms (see Section 1.4, "Six Sigma"). This is important because new processes are often not optimized relative to meeting the business goals of an organization. There is an old saying that it is possible to create "concrete life preservers" using systematic process improvement models. This is because the process must first exist before it can be improved and then optimized. A shocking revelation in the early days of implementing the CMM for Software (1985-1990) is that most software organizations were a "mud sucking" level 1 in their process maturity, which meant that their processes were not defined. Thus, the first priority was to focus on defining these processes within the business framework of the organization. In general, the appraisal models do not judge the quality of process but are more interested in whether the process exists, is documented, and is instantiated—

Table 1-3: *Mapping of LAI Enabling Practices to CMMI*

LAI Enabling Practices (from Lean Enterprise Model)	CMMI Specific Practices, Specific Goals, and Process Areas (PAs)	CMMI Generic Practices and Goals and Maturity or Capability Levels
Systems Engineering Approach	Engineering PAs	Levels 2 & 3
Requirements	RM, RD	Levels 2 & 3
Design for Mfg, Support . . .	RM, TS	Level 3
Inspections	PPQA, Peer Review Goal in VER	Level 2
Planning	PP, IPM, QPM	Level 2
Risk Management	RSKM	Level 3
Data Management	PM	Level 2
IPTs	IPPD Extension	Level 3
Stakeholder Involvement	Throughout	Level 2
Skills and Training	OT	Level 2
Software Factory	Engineering PAs	Levels 2 & 3
Metrics	MA, QPM	Levels 2, 3, & 4
Define Processes	OPD	Levels 2 & 3
Model Process Flow	OPD	Levels 2 & 3
Data and Root Causes	QPM, CAR	Levels 2, 3, & 4 (Data) and Level 5 (Root Causes)
Variability Reduction	QPM	Levels 4 & 5
Improvement Targets	OID	Level 5
Continually Improve Processes	CAR, OID	Level 5

this is especially true at lower levels of maturity. As organizations reach higher levels of CMMI maturity where statistical control processes are enforced, this issue becomes less apparent.

The cultural time it takes to accept appraisal results from LESAT versus SCAMPI is different. Lean evolved out of the manufacturing world, a world with complex proprietary processes that have had a lot of attention over the years. As a result, systematic process improvement principles are easier to accept within the manufacturing-oriented culture where Lean had its heritage. Alternatively, in the software world, although the processes are comparatively simple (that is, usually the number of steps is smaller), the creative culture in the systems and software engineering communities did not initially relate as well to process improvement. LAI was created to reduce the cost of producing aircraft, and thus initially focused on production. Since the industrial revolution, firms have been developing and improving their production processes, methods, and tools, and process improvement is an accepted mechanism within many manufacturing-oriented organizations. Given the success of process management in manufacturing operations, senior management is usually more open to applying these principles to other parts of the organization. CMMI is focused on the creative process of developing software-intensive systems, and there is a natural countervailing force on being able to adequately capture intellectual versus operational processes. As more firms reach higher levels of CMMI process maturity, this resistance should decrease.

1.4 Six Sigma

Six Sigma is a popular improvement methodology developed and used by Motorola Corporation, Texas Instruments, and many other companies. This section discusses the Six Sigma philosophy and process, and it shows how Six Sigma might be incorporated into a CMMI improvement and appraisal effort.[18]

---

[18] There are many good books about Six Sigma. One of them is *Implementing Six Sigma: Smarter Solutions Using Statistical Methods, Second Edition*, by F. Breyfogle (John Wiley & Sons, Hoboken, NJ, 2003).

Six Sigma is a term that applies to a method and a measure. It has evolved from the work of several quality notables—Genechi Taguchi, Bill Smith, Philip Crosby, W. Edwards Deming, and Walter A. Shewhart, to name a few. There is no single governing body for Six Sigma. The fundamental objective of the Six Sigma methodology is the implementation of a measurement-based strategy that focuses on process improvement and variation reduction through the application of Six Sigma improvement projects.

Six Sigma has four major objectives:

1. Maintain control of process
2. Improve constantly
3. Exceed customer's expectations
4. Add tangibly to the bottom line

Six Sigma brings with it several tools, such as error mode and effect analysis, regression analysis, process simulation, and control charts. These tools are useful in improving processes to satisfy CMMI. That said, there is a difference with respect to the use of tools. Within the CMMI Framework, tools are not prescriptive, although it is necessary to use statistical tools at the higher capability and maturity levels. Tools within the Six Sigma Framework are proscribed and sequenced, and there is an explicit use of statistical tools.

Six Sigma, along with its tools, can advance CMMI's objectives—these two process improvement mechanisms do not compete. Both are bottom-up methods of continuous improvement. Six Sigma is more focused on a project team and CMMI is more focused on organizational processes. Unlike the model-based approaches to process improvement, such as CMMI and Lean, Six Sigma does not include any process models. It is a strategy to improve the bottom line coupled with a measurement-driven method for continuous improvement. In Six Sigma, individual processes are selected based on their capability to affect business results and provide visible value to the customer. The connection between process performance measurement and business is always explicit at the project level, so it is comparatively easy to measure *return on investment* (ROI). CMMI is more focused on having the organizational processes defined, codified, and institutionalized. Like Lean, Six Sigma evolved out of the manufacturing world, a world with operational processes that, although complex, have been well studied. This is in contrast with CMMI, which evolved out of the creative world of software and systems engineering, a world of intellectual processes that are difficult to optimize given the variability of the human intellect.

A widely accepted cliché is that Six Sigma isn't appropriate for software until an organization is level 4 or level 5. The Six Sigma toolkit aligns nicely with the quantitative process management, product quality management, and process optimization practices associated with CMMI levels 4 and 5. Unfortunately many organizations never even reach level 4 or 5 because the maturity models allow them to avoid a sharp focus on the bottom line through level 3. This would not be an issue if an organization could move to level 4 in a year or two, but typical organizations reach the higher maturity levels so slowly, if ever, that they lose focus along the way. CMMI recognizes these issues to some extent. It has a process area called *Measurement and Analysis* (MA) staged at maturity level 2, which makes it difficult to defer putting a measurement framework in place early on. This brings it somewhat closer into alignment with Six Sigma at the lower maturity levels.

Combining Six Sigma at the tactical level with model-based improvement at the strategic level provides the best of both worlds. Six Sigma and CMMI-based process improvement are complementary: Six Sigma strengthens analysis capabilities and CMMI provides organizational structure. Six Sigma analysis techniques can be used to establish priorities for selecting individual process for improvement within CMMI's continuous improvement model, or at every level of CMMI's staged model. The process maturity model provides a strategic framework for continuous improvement, a perspective on industry best practices, and a systematic approach to benchmarking. This avoids excessive analysis, reinventing the wheel, and inadvertent suboptimization.

Here's an example of how Six Sigma might be incorporated into a CMMI improvement and appraisal effort: Raytheon uses an integrated three-part process strategy to ensure that its corporate business goals map to its product development, program management, and customer satisfaction measures. It ties together its life cycle development process, CMMI, and Six Sigma. The overarching element of this strategy is Raytheon's use of Six Sigma. The philosophies and guidelines of Six Sigma are further instantiated in the more detailed Integrated Product Development System, used as the corporate guide for doing business, developing products, and serving customers. The CMMI Framework serves to solidify the integration of systems, software engineering, and other disciplines prescribed in its life cycle development system. The net result is an integrated framework with optimized processes that meet its business goals.

1.5 ISO 9000

ISO 9000 is actually a family of standards that represents good management practices to ensure an organization can consistently deliver products or services that meet its customers' quality requirements. This is the same primary objective that CMMI addresses. In fact, CMMI is a set of best practices that ensures satisfactory performance when practiced at increasing levels of capability. This section discusses the common features of ISO 9000 and CMMI.[19]

The family of ISO quality standards includes

* ISO 9000:2000, *guidelines*
* ISO 9001:2000, *requirements*
* ISO 9004:2000, *guidelines*

Because ISO 9001 represents the process requirements, it is the primary CMMI-related document. It contains the requirements for five areas:

* Quality Management Systems
* Management responsibility
* Resource Management
* Product realization
* Measurement, analysis, and improvement

Each of these areas contains requirements that can be traced to practices in CMMI. Table 1-4 shows a condensation of the major sections traced at the process area level. Other than the generic practices listed in Table 1-4, we do not provide traces to other CMMI practices.

Table 1-4 shows that there is considerable commonality between ISO 9001:2000 and CMMI. There are a few requirements in ISO 9001:2000 that are not covered in CMMI, and some are not as explicit in one as in the other. In some cases CMMI is more explicit and provides more details than ISO 9001:2000. The opposite is true as well.

---

[19] The International Organization for Standardization (ISO) provides information about ISO 9000 documents on its website: http://www.iso.org/iso/en/iso9000-14000/iso9000/iso9000index. html.

Table 1-4: *Mapping of ISO 9001 to CMMI*

Section	*ISO 9001 Title*	*CMMI PA, Generic Practice*
4	*Quality Management System*	
4.1	General requirements	OPF, OPD
4.2	Documentation requirements	OPF, OPD, CM, GP 2.6
5	*Management responsibility*	
5.1	Management commitment	GP 2.1
5.2	Customer focus	RD, GP 2.7
5.3	Quality policy	OPF, GP 2.1
5.4	Planning	OPF, OPD, OPP, GP 2.2
5.5	Responsibility, authority, and communication	GP 2.4
5.6	Management review	OPF, PMC, GP 2.10
6	*Resource Management*	
6.1	Provision of resources	GP 2.3
6.2	Human resources	OT, OEI, GP 2.3
6.3	Infrastructure	OEI
6.4	Work environment	OEI, PP
7	*Product realization*	
7.1	Planning product realization	OPD, PP, IPM, GP 2.2
7.2	Customer-related processes	REQM, RD, TS, VER
7.3	Design and development	PP, PMC, CM, IPM, RD, TS, PI, VER, VAL
7.4	Purchasing	SAM, TS, ISM
7.5	Production and service provision	RD, TS, PI, VAL, CM
7.6	Control and monitoring of measuring devices	VER, VAL, MA

Section	ISO 9001 Title	CMMI PA, Generic Practice
8	*Measurement, analysis, and improvement*	
8.1	General	MA, QPM
8.3	Control of nonconforming product	MA, PMC, PPQA, OPF, OPD, VAL, VER
8.4	Analysis of data	CM, PMC, MA, RD, QPM, GP 3.2
8.5	Improvement	PMC, MA, OPF, CAR

In general terms, an organization that satisfies CMMI will also satisfy ISO 9001:2000. However, the conservative approach is to ensure that the organization's processes satisfy both ISO 9001:2000's requirements and CMMI's goals by tracing the process elements to both. There is sufficient commonality between CMMI and ISO that interest is developing to explore whether a single appraisal could satisfy both CMMI and ISO 9001:2000.

ISO 9001 audits are performed on an organization to ensure that the quality objectives and practices are met by an organization. These audits result in a certificate indicating that the organization is 9001 compliant. Normally, audits are performed every six months, with re-certification in three years.

1.6 Agile

Agile methods provide a means of streamlining development and manufacturing processes into their most fundamental and critical components. Organizations must balance their need for agility with the benefits of having standardized processes. This section reviews the Agile approach and how it might compete with or complement model-based process improvement and process appraisals.[20]

---

[20] For a discussion of how Agile methods may be of use in an organization working to improve its processes, see *Balancing Agility and Discipline: A Guide for the Perplexed* (B. Boehm and Turner, R., Pearson Education, Boston, MA, 2003).

What exactly does it mean to be more agile? Merriam-Webster defines agile as *marked by ready ability to move with quick easy grace*. Sounds like a good thing, but it isn't a word typically used to describe software projects. Words like *predictable*, *cost-effective*, and *mature* are more often used to characterize desirable development processes.

The rapid evolution of market, customer need, and technology causes a demand for the quicker delivery of useful systems, increasingly vague and volatile requirements, and greater uncertainty and risk from many sources. These include a less-than-complete knowledge of underlying technologies, *off-the-shelf* (OTS) components used, and domain challenges and tradeoffs. Agile thinking begins with that stark economic perspective: There can be no return on investment until the system starts operating. Consequently, developers are compelled to get some sort of system of at least some value to the customer in operation as soon as possible. Further, developers think they should continue to deliver system updates of maximum value in minimum time.

Conventional wisdom has focused on systematic process improvement (such as CMMI) as a way to address quality, productivity, risk, and progress for software-intensive projects. CMMI imposes a disciplined process on software development with the aim of making software development more predictable and more efficient. It does this by requiring detailed processes. Proponents of an Agile approach may criticize the CMMI saying that it produces processes that are bureaucratic. There are so many requirements that the whole pace of development slows down. Often it is perception that rules the day.

As a reaction to the systematic process improvement models, a new group of methodologies has appeared in the last few years, especially focused on software. For a while these were known as "lightweight" methodologies, but now the accepted term is "Agile" methodologies. For many people the appeal of these Agile methodologies is their reaction to the perceived bureaucracy of the systematic process improvement models. These new methods attempt a useful compromise between "no process" and "too much process," providing just enough process to gain a reasonable payoff. Developers sense that short delivery cycles enable them to stay on target with the customer's changing value criteria.

Critics have raised serious issues about Agile development: It is just an excuse to "hack," Agile can't scale up to large projects, Agile can't work with distributed teams, Agile can't handle serious architectural issues, and customers and developers won't work that way. Although each of these criticisms can be addressed, they are barriers to the acceptance of Agile methodologies.

The Agile Alliance has described the attributes of Agile development methodologies.[21] The attributes include the following:

- Deliver working, valuable software early and frequently
- Measure progress primarily by working software
- Have business people and developers work together daily
- Welcome changing requirements
- Create a self-organizing team of motivated individuals
- Communicate using face-to-face conversation
- Avoid nonessential work
- Maintain a sustainable pace of development
- Attend continuously to good design
- Retrospect and adjust regularly

In short, a profound shift in mindset distinguishes Agile development from conventional approaches heavy on planning and upfront analysis. As expressed by the Agile Alliance, Agile development emphasizes

- *Individuals and interactions* over processes and tools
- *Working software* over comprehensive documentation
- *Customer collaboration* over contract negotiation
- *Responding to change* over following a plan

While they recognize value in the items on the right, they value the items on the left more.

Agile development regards system development primarily as a learning process. This perception alters the conventional risk and benefit tradeoff. For example, detailed planning for the long-term is seen as having little value; the details (at least) will undoubtedly change as the project team learns more during the early delivery cycles. Similarly, Agile development prefers to substitute frequent, informal person-to-person (and optimally, face-to-face) interaction for formal textual or graphical documents, which always fail to be comprehensive and are impossible to maintain at an appropriate rate of change the closer they

---

[21] From "Principles Behind the Agile Manifesto" at www.agilealliance.org/principles.html.

come to being comprehensive. Both planned delivery approaches based on the CMMI and also Agile methodologies are being used. However, projects still go over budget and schedule, and requirements are often not met; thus, neither of these approaches is a cure-all for delivering quality software that meets customer requirements on time and on schedule. It can be reasonably argued that these approaches are being used to deal with issues such as customer needs that change, rapid technology evolution that is accelerating, increasing speed of market shifts, and the need to develop increasingly sophisticated systems to address increasingly complex problems. A key issue is how they relate and when to use one or the other.

Both the planned delivery development and Agile method approach are responses to the problems associated with software hacking. Figure 1-5 contrasts the three approaches: Planned Delivery Deployment, which is associated with CMMI, Agile Methodology, and Hacking.

Given the need for quality, most projects can benefit from increased agility as well as a planned delivery development approach (versus in the case of software, hacking). Both approaches are interested in delivering systems and software that meet the customer requirements. As the size and complexity of a project grows (measured by the number of system requirements, major interfaces, operational scenarios, critical algorithms, and so on), Agile development becomes more challenging. In such cases a planned delivery development is often the preferred development approach; it is in this realm that CMMI is most effective.

Boehm and Turner point out that Agile versus plan-driven analysis are not absolutely in conflict; they can be treated as two ends of a continuum to be managed on the basis of a risk.[22] Consider Figure 1-6, derived from a similar figure by Cockburn. Agile development fits most easily with small (fewer than 50 developers), non-life-critical projects. On the other hand, on larger or life-critical projects, the advantages of heavy upfront planning and analysis outweigh its disadvantages as project logistics become very complicated or the customer's willingness to tolerate defects in the delivered system decreases.

However, a large project need not be wholly planned or wholly Agile. Where there is considerable experience with and understanding of a large or complicated system element, or safety or correct operation is otherwise at a premium, extended planning and analysis may be the

---

[22] Boehm and Turner, p. 100.

best strategy. More volatile or less understood system elements deserve a more agile treatment. Alternately, select development subteams for Agile practice based on their size and cultural outlook. Overall, the benefits of Agile techniques are much constrained using a piecemeal approach, but will be an improvement over ignoring agility entirely.

In summary, CMMI can be applied to a large class of software-intensive efforts. As projects become more complex and increase in size, Agile methods are less applicable and a planned delivery approach contained in CMMI is often the preferred approach. At the present time, SCAMPI is constrained by CMMI and would have to be tailored before appraising projects that are using Agile developmental methodologies.

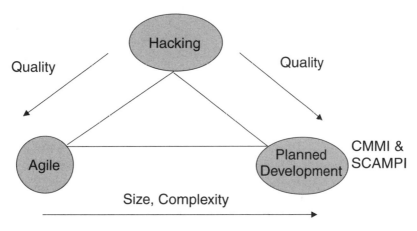

Figure 1-5: *Agile, CMMI, and Hacking*

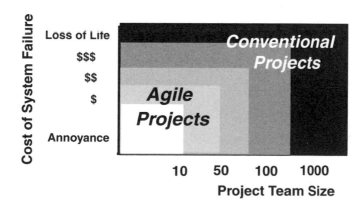

Figure 1-6: *Area of Dominance for Agile Versus Conventional Development*

1.7 Integrating Appraisal Efforts

Having reviewed CMMI, together with Lean, ISO 9000, Six Sigma, and Agile, it is clear that organizations will have a complex task putting it all together and finding a viable path to process improvement, quality, customer satisfaction, and business success. We close this introductory chapter with reflections on some things to consider as you travel this path. Here we speak not to the details of the various approaches, but more generally of the integration of process improvement across an enterprise.

As management practices have evolved over the past decade, organizations have learned that to be successful they must become adept at continuously defining and redefining their direction and objectives—organizational agility has become a guiding principle of successful companies. They must also develop a means of measuring the degree to which their objectives are being achieved. During the 1980s, concerns about American competitiveness steered many U.S. companies to a new interest in quality. Three leading "quality gurus" were W. Edwards Deming, Joseph Juran, and Philip Crosby. To quote Deming, "Improvement of the process increases uniformity of product, reduces rework and mistakes, reduces waste of manpower, machine-time, and materials, and thus, increases output with less effort. Other benefits of improved quality are lower costs . . . happier people on the job and more jobs, through better competitive position of the company."[23] Traditional performance measures are being employed to display financial performance, operational efficiency, and so on. However, these traditional measures inadequately portray progress toward achieving behavioral changes and in showing the effectiveness of comprehensive improvement strategies. As we have seen, a variety of appraisal tools have emerged that facilitate initiatives aimed at implementing continual improvement strategies.

Appraisal processes are imbedded in several of the process improvement frameworks and models. Given that an appraisal method covers the scope of a process improvement model, the issues associated with the implementation of process improvement models are similar to those associated with implementation of the process improvement frameworks. Most organizations within an enterprise have built a

---

[23] From a presentation made by Deming at the Software Engineering Institute, Carnegie Mellon University, as part of the introduction of the CMM for Software.

process infrastructure at the organizational level. While the components of the infrastructure remain the same, additional challenges are introduced when the infrastructure is developed at the enterprise level. Process improvement models may overlap each other at the enterprise level; thus, there can be multiple appraisals of the same practice if different appraisal models are used. To resolve this issue, organizations have developed process architectures. A process architecture describes the ordering, interfaces, interdependencies, and other relationships among the process elements in a standard process. Process architecture also describes the interfaces, interdependencies, and other relationships between process elements and external processes (for example, contract management).

In order to expand business markets and improve quality, productivity, predictability, and cost, enterprises have defined and improved their processes to be compliant with one or more frameworks and have hopefully resolved many of the differences via process architectures. That said, because of framework limitations and focus, parallel processes have been developed and maintained within the enterprise. Engineering disciplines developed frameworks (such as the CMM for Software, EIA 731, and CMMI) aligned to their disciplines. Acquisitions and mergers have even introduced process duplication into enterprises where framework compliance among the organizations is the same.

Recently, integrated frameworks have been developed that combine several discipline-specific frameworks. In addition to CMMI, there is the *Federal Aviation Administration-Integrated Capability Maturity Model* (FAA-iCMM). Both CMMI and iCMM encourage integration of processes across the enterprise and attempt to alleviate the need for multiple framework appraisals. Although each provides a broader scope, neither of these frameworks has totally eliminated the need for measuring compliance with multiple frameworks.

The introduction of broader frameworks and the realized cost and inefficiencies of maintaining independent parallel processes across the enterprise have motivated many enterprises to develop integrated multicompliant processes. However, moving to an enterprisewide, integrated multicompliant process is a highly complex undertaking. There are organizational, managerial, and business issues as well as technical issues.

Process improvement with an integrated model like CMMI does not by itself imply the existence of integrated processes. What needs to be developed is a strategy for integrated multicompliant processes derived from business objectives. Figure 1-7 shows the steps in establishing the strategy. A description of each follows:

Quantifying business goals. The enterprise business objectives form the basis for setting quantifiable benefits as a result of achieving integrated multicompliant processes. These goals assist in determining the scope of enterprise involvement.

Defining the enterprise's integrated multicompliant strategy. The enterprise defines the strategy, mapping framework compliance to organizations within the enterprise, and defining the level of process integration across the enterprise. The strategy includes the timetable for each organization to achieve compliance to the identified frameworks.

Performing a cost-benefit analysis of the strategy. A business case analysis translates the cost and benefits of the strategy into ROI. Enterprises use this technique to refine the strategy.

Identifying and analyzing risks. The enterprise identifies the key risks associated with developing integrated multicompliant processes across the enterprise and makes recommendations for mitigating these risks.

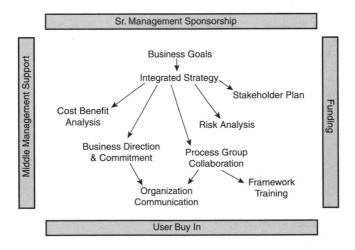

Figure 1-7: *Establishing the Strategy*

Developing the stakeholder collaboration plan. In this plan, the enterprise identifies all stakeholders and plans for active collaboration of organizations across the enterprise. The plan also details periodic and ongoing communication that will be used throughout the effort.

When an appraisal covers multiple disciplines within its scope (such as systems and software), there are several complexities and risks that exist when compared with a single-discipline appraisal. The integrated approach to multicompliant processes includes risks similar to any large process improvement initiative. Among these common process improvement risks, those that are generally considered high probability and high consequence in an integrated multicompliant process initiative are detailed in the following paragraphs.

Maintaining senior management participation and sponsorship. Maintaining sustained participation and sponsorship throughout the effort is essential. If the effort ceases to be viewed as top priority through continued senior management discussion and involvement, the effort is viewed by the enterprise as unimportant. This scenario generally results in failure. There are several areas where senior management participation is required, and making this participation and sponsorship visible throughout the enterprise is a key to mitigating this risk.

Sustaining collaboration among the process team members. In enterprises where multiple process teams were established along discipline or framework boundaries, there may be strong resistance to moving toward an integrated process. Management needs to understand the concerns and actively solicit and direct collaboration among the members of the process group.

Maintaining funding throughout the effort. Funding needs are derived from the cost-benefit analysis and can be tracked against performance of the effort.

Eliciting middle management support. In many organizations, middle management has primarily been focused on meeting program cost and schedules. Implementation of the Enterprise Framework Strategy places time and resource demands on middle management; these demands are often perceived as contrary to their goals. The importance of their participation can be emphasized by including attainment of the Enterprise Framework as a measured task on their performance objectives.

Creating process user buy-in. Process users are typically resistant to process change, particularly if they do not perceive added value. Integration of processes to be compliant with multiple frameworks can be viewed as change for change's sake. The time lost to training and gaining experience with new tools and processes creates resistance among many process users. There are several ways to mitigate this risk. A recognized approach is having process users who have influence within their organizations participate in the needed process definition and redefinition. Awareness of senior management sponsorship and involvement adds credence to the importance.

Assuring that diverse organizations understand each other. The larger and more diverse the enterprise, the more difficult it is to establish communication and integration. Lack of familiarity with each other's businesses focuses discussion on differences and uniqueness, slowing the progress toward integration. Wherever possible, including people in the process groups that have a broad experience and knowledge base helps mitigate this risk.

Gaining knowledge of multiple frameworks. Expertise in frameworks is often limited to expertise in one framework. Because the Enterprise Framework Strategy requires compliance with several frameworks, determining process requirements against several frameworks requires a working knowledge of all frameworks in the Enterprise Framework. Lack of sufficient knowledge and experience with all frameworks in the Enterprise Framework results in delays and can produce inaccuracies. If multiframework expertise is absent within the enterprise, the enterprise may choose to seek external help to provide guidance for processes that need to satisfy several frameworks or provide basic training for all frameworks to the process groups included in the endeavor.

Analyzing current business directions and commitments. Current commitments and direction may introduce additional risk with respect to resource availability and timeframes. In some cases, they may present hard constraints to the integrated process effort. In either case, analysis by top management is needed to determine whether timeframes identified in the strategy need to be modified or directions need to be changed.

These represent the most commonly encountered risks. The size, diversity of business models, and geographic dispersion within an enterprise all increase the probability and consequence of the risks. All risks need to be identified, analyzed, monitored, and controlled throughout the transition effort. When the probability of risk mitigation is low, the enterprise may choose to limit the scope of enterprise involvement or postpone some activities, if possible, until success with risks of lower consequence has been realized. A *Risk Management Plan* (RMP) is the typical vehicle for managing risks.

1.8 Summary

In this chapter we have taken a broad look at process appraisal strategies, reviewing CMMI, Lean, Six Sigma, ISO 9000, and Agile, and closing with reflections on a strategy to integrate business processes across an enterprise. CMMI is only one source of process requirements in an organization. Processes should be structured to meet the requirements of customers and applicable standards, as well as selected process improvement models. As you read the chapters that follow and learn more about CMMI and the SCAMPI appraisal methods, always keep in mind how you best can use what CMMI offers in the larger context of the other approaches to process improvement that are followed in your organization.

Part II

SCAMPI Appraisals

After the dishes have been prepared and the guests are seated at the table, if you wait too long to serve them you may hear the question, "Where's the beef?" Or, if the menu is seafood you may of course hear instead, "Where's the shrimp?" In any case, keeping diners waiting too long can lead either to impatience or boredom. Similarly, when readers pick up a book on process appraisals, the authors should not keep them waiting too long to get to the meat of the subject. Having examined in Part I, "Why SCAMPI Now?", the menu of process appraisal options, we now turn to the details of the CMMI SCAMPI appraisal methods. Here is where you discover the best ways to use these appraisals so that they meet the needs of your organization, without giving you indigestion.

Part II Contents

Chapter 4. SCAMPI Class B and C Appraisal Methods

The less rigorous and less costly versions of the SCAMPI method, "Class B" and "Class C," may be used to develop process improvement plans and (perhaps) to prepare an organization for a full-scale Class A SCAMPI appraisal.

Chapter 5. SCAMPI for Internal Process Improvement

We highlight for those wanting to use SCAMPI for internal process improvement or for an internal organizational benchmark some aspects of the method that may be new or deserve emphasis, including preparation, the appraisal team, and the appraisal timeline.

Chapter 6. SCAMPI for External Audits

Some of the issues that arise when a SCAMPI appraisal is used for an external audit or evaluation, including a government source selection, the selection of suppliers, and contract monitoring.

Chapter 2

New Aspects of the SCAMPI Method

shrimp scam·pi an appraisal whose scope includes only a
very small number of the CMMI process areas

chick·en scam·pi an appraisal whose lead appraiser comes
from within the organization being appraised

In this chapter, we briefly review several of the major factors that drove
the development of the SCAMPI appraisal method. For readers who
have some familiarity with legacy appraisal methods, such as CBA-IPI
and the EIA 731 method, this may be useful as you transition to the
SCAMPI method. For all readers, as you work toward an in-depth
understanding of the SCAMPI method, keep these factors in mind
along with why things are the way they are and how you can best make
use of it.

2.1 From Discovery to Verification

The integrated CMMI models combine the materials from three legacy
models; the disciplines addressed include software, systems engineering, and integrated process and product development. Therefore, it is no
surprise that the size of the integrated model, an amalgam that covers all
three areas, is larger than any one of the single-discipline legacy models.
With a larger model, there is more to review during an appraisal. One of

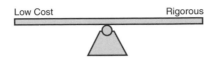

Figure 2-1: *Balancing Low Cost and Rigorous Benchmarking*

the primary objectives of the SCAMPI development was to maintain the quality of the legacy appraisals but at the same time keep the cost of a CMMI SCAMPI appraisal lower than the combined cost of multiple single-discipline appraisals. Several methods were evaluated by the Product Development Team to address the expanded size of the CMMI models; the goal was to keep cost within reasonable limits and at the same time retain a rigorous benchmarking capability. These two objectives were in competition on the opposite ends of a teeter-totter. It was a challenge to keep these two objectives balanced during the development of SCAMPI and it remains so at present.

The CBA-IPI assessment method, which was used with the CMM for Software, was considered a rigorous benchmarking method. However, it was based on the "discovery" of evidence by an assessment team that the goals of the model were indeed satisfied. This was a very labor-intensive process. The team was responsible for finding evidence that each activity was satisfied through a review of documents and interviews. The developers of CMMI and its appraisal methods determined that the time required discovering that all of the CMMI goals were satisfied in the style of the CBA-IPI method would be excessive with a large model like CMMI.

In addition, some believed that the CBA-IPI method allowed for too much variability. Given the same organization, how consistently could different CBA-IPI teams reach the same conclusions on the model satisfaction? The developers of the method considered consistency of appraisal findings to be an important objective of the new CMMI appraisal method. They strove for a low-cost benchmarking method where there was a high probability that different SCAMPI teams would reach the same findings for an organization.

The basis of the solution to these challenges was to create a "verification" appraisal method rather than a discovery method. With a verification method, the organization undergoing the appraisal is responsible for providing traces from the model's goals and practices to the evidence generated by the processes that they use. The appraisal team then verifies that what the organization has provided is valid for each practice. While this reduces the appraisal team's effort, a SCAMPI appraisal is still neither easy nor quick. There are ongoing challenges to further reduce the cost of applying the method while maintaining the benchmarking capabilities of the method.

2.2 Focused Investigations

Large amounts of objective evidence are necessary due to the size of the CMMI model, the disciplines covered, and SCAMPI method rules. Efficient appraisals require effective data collection and management strategies. Focused investigations are used to track and prioritize appraisal team effort on the data that may still be needed for sufficient coverage of model practices within the appraisal scope. The appraisal team must continually keep in mind the following questions: What data do I have? What data do I still need? How am I going to collect the data? If the organization has prepared properly, the appraisal team's effort to verify the processes is much easier. How does the organization deal with the large amount of data required by the team to verify the processes?

Let's take a look at the amount of data to be collected and verified for an organization that is appraising three projects against the CMMI-SE/SW/IPPD/SS. There are 185 specific practices in this model (staged representation). Each specific practice requires at least one direct evidence data item.[1] Some practices may require more. This model has 25 process areas for maturity level 5, so the generic practice direct evidence may include at least one item of data for each GP for each process area. Table 2-1 summarizes the number of data items for each project.

The appraisal team also looks for indirect evidence or affirmations for each practice. To reduce the risk of not satisfying the desired maturity level rating, let's assume that the organization and projects collect at least one indirect evidence data item for each practice. (Although this is not required by the SCAMPI method, the organization being appraised may feel safer by providing to the appraisal team indirect evidence

---

[1] See section 3.3.5 for a discussion of the difference between direct and indirect evidence in a SCAMPI appraisal. Briefly, if you prepare a dish following a recipe, the dish itself is the direct evidence that you prepared it and followed (more or less) the recipe, whereas the receipts for the ingredients and a food-spattered copy of the recipe would be examples of indirect evidence.

Table 2-1: *Data Items Required for Each Project (ML5)*

	Direct Evidence	Indirect Evidence	Total
Specific practices	185	185	370
Generic practices	300	300	600
Total	**485**	**485**	**970**

data items for all practices.) This doubles the amount of data needed for the appraisal.

This adds up to a minimum of about 1,000 data items for a single project and 3,000 data items for three projects. In reality, there could be an even larger number needed to ensure that the appraisal team can verify each practice for each project. For example, some practices are compound sentences and a single data item may not satisfy the verification needs of the team. For instance, take GP 3.2: *Collect work products, measures, measurement results, and improvement information derived from planning and performing the process to support the future use and improvement of the organization's processes and process assets.* It might be difficult to create a process work product that shows all these expectations for a process area. More than likely, a measurement repository output will be needed as well as example work products in the process asset library or libraries, reports, and lessons learned. This GP is needed for every PA within the scope of the appraisal. Add these data items and their indirect evidence items and the number of data items to be collected for each project can easily approach 1,500 to 1,700. This results in 4,500 to 5,100 data items to be collected and verified for a three-project appraisal at maturity level 5.

An undeniable conclusion: It is a significant task for the organization and its projects to manage the collection and presentation of this large number of data items.

However, it should be noted that these data items reflect the results of work performed by the project or organization. Thus, a high-maturity organization that would be striving for maturity level 5 does not have to create them—it just has to find them. This is the collection of work products that are the natural consequence of the organization and its projects following their defined processes. The task is to organize the data and map it to the model practices. While this is still a significant undertaking, one side effect of the effort may be the sharing of lessons learned across projects and across disciplines, which can support future process improvement efforts.

Please remember that requiring indirect artifacts for every practice is not required, and in many cases affirmations may be a much more efficient way to corroborate the direct artifacts.

Some organizations use hard copies of each data item and create indexes to the library. This was a common practice in CBA-IPI assessments. However, the larger amount of data required for CMMI is driving the need for automated libraries and online access to the data items. Some organizations have created databases that provide links to the files on servers or web sites that contain the data items. Others have created web sites that control the access to the same types of information. There are also tools provided by software development companies and consulting organizations to be used by their clients.

2.3 For EIA 731 Users

The appraisal method in EIA 731[2]—*Systems Engineering Capability Model* (SECM)—is quite different from the CBA-IPI method in some respects, but in others it is very similar. If you listened in on a group of EIA 731 appraisers, you would hear them talking about questionnaires, interviews, and focus area ratings. The SCAMPI appraisers would be talking about document reviews, interviews, and either process area capability level ratings or maturity level ratings. EIA 731 is primarily an affirmation process rather than a discovery process or a verification process. The EIA 731 method uses questionnaires to collect data. The team evaluates the questionnaires and then interviews the participants to fill gaps in what was affirmed by the questionnaires. Next, they rate the practices within the focus areas and roll up the data to themes and focus areas.

Some of the EIA 731 appraisal features have been combined with the CBA-IPI method to define the SCAMPI method. However, SCAMPI is much closer to the CBA-IPI than the EIA 731 method. One of the reasons for this is that the EIA 731 method was not written for third-party

[2] The EIA 731 Appraisal Method was developed by the G47 SECM Working Group of the Government Electronics & Information Technology Association (GEIA).

evaluations or benchmarking appraisals. One of the SCAMPI requirements is that it can be used for these purposes. In fact, the EIA 731
method says that it is not to be used for that purpose (like LESAT,
described in Section 1.3 of Chapter 1, "Process Appraisal Strategies").
Performing benchmarks requires more rigor in the appraisal than that
provided by the EIA 731 method. On the other hand, the EIA 731
method provided the affirmation features of the SCAMPI approach.

The phases of an EIA 731 appraisal and the primary outputs of the EIA
731 appraisal are the same as that of the SCAMPI. The phases are called
Preparation, On-site, and Post Appraisal in EIA 731, and Plan and Prepare for Appraisal, Conduct Appraisal, and Report Results in SCAMPI.
The most significant difference in the phases is in the preparation
phase. In EIA 731 preparation, the participants complete a questionnaire and attend interview and feedback sessions. In preparing for
SCAMPI, the programs being appraised prepare objective evidence for
every practice within the scope of the appraisal. This can be a very
expensive and time-consuming activity. In comparing the two methods, EIA 732 is nearer the low cost end of the teeter-totter while
SCAMPI is nearer the rigorous end.

The primary outputs for both methods are findings and a rating report.
The ratings report produced by EIA 731 is in the form of a capability
profile. See Figure 2-2 for an example EIA 731 profile. A scoring profile
is also an optional output of the SCAMPI. One key difference in the
scoring is that in an EIA 731 appraisal, partial credit for satisfaction of a
focus area is given. Notice in the example profile in Figure 2-2 that the
scores provide the capability to score the focus areas at 1.5, 2.5, and so
on. SCAMPI only allows full satisfaction of capability levels.

The SCAMPI method provides a very good mechanism for doing par-
tially satisfied (more informative) charts by reporting the ratings at the
practice and goal levels as well as the process area, but this level of
graphing is not done. The information would be available in the findings report, and an organization could create such charts after the
appraisal team leaves. The advantage of this charting method is that
the organization can see at a glance what the weaknesses are. Of
course, if the organization asks for a maturity level rating it may get
just a number and no profile at all.

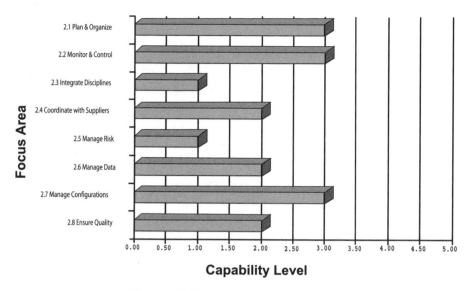

Figure 2-2: *Example EIA 731 Profile*

Profile Use

The *Australia Ministry of Defense* (AMOD) uses profiles instead of maturity level ratings in their acquisition selection process. Just as an organization can create profiles to meet their business needs as efficiently as possible, the AMOD uses them to meet their acquisition needs. This allows them to expect higher capability in key areas than in areas that are not as critical given the situation for the acquisition.

2.4 Summary

The authors of SCAMPI have worked to balance the cost and rigor of the method. SCAMPI was developed from the CMM for Software's CBA-IPI method and the SECM method; one very rigorous and one very cost effective. This balance of cost and rigor has been accomplished (in part) by basing the SCAMPI appraisal method on verification of data rather than on discovery. One consequence of this is that the organization is responsible for presenting a large amount of data to the appraisal team for them to verify. A vehicle to communicate how the data from the organization being appraised relates to the model is the Practice Implementation Indicator Description (PIID). PIIDs and the Class A SCAMPI method are discussed in the next chapter.

Chapter 3

SCAMPI Class A Method Definition

prune scam·pi an appraisal whose team members are retirees
split pea scam·pi an appraisal that generates distinct
ratings for software and systems engineering

3.1 Background

As we noted earlier in section 1.1, SCAMPI is a combination of appraisal techniques from the CBA-IPI and EIA 731-2 appraisal methods. These methods were created at different times, to support appraisals of two distinct disciplines (software and systems engineering), based on models with divergent architectural structures (staged and continuous). Nonetheless in many respects, these two appraisal methods are very similar. They both address three types of source information—artifacts, instruments, and interviews—but in varying ways and with differing emphasis. They each include the development of findings and getting feedback on those findings from the organization being appraised; they each provide "rules of the road" that the appraisal team must follow on how to reach conclusions. However, each has its own twist. The SCAMPI authors combined these two methods and took best practices from each in order to create a more effective and efficient method.

Prior to creating the SCAMPI method, the CMMI Team developed a document entitled *Appraisal Requirements for CMMI (ARC)*, which we mentioned earlier in section 1.2(c). The ARC contains basic requirements and design criteria for appraisal methods based on the CMMI models. To a large extent the ARC itself is based on the original *CMM Appraisal Framework* (CAF) that drives the CBA-IPI method.[1] The ARC distinguishes three classes of appraisal: Class A, Class B, and Class C. In this chapter we focus on the SCAMPI Class A method, which is the most rigorous and permits the appraisal team to assign capability and maturity level ratings. See Chapter 4, "SCAMPI Class B and C Appraisal Methods," for a presentation of less rigorous SCAMPI Class B and Class C methods.

The initial SCAMPI version 1.0 was very similar to a CBA-IPI, with the addition of a structured instrument for written, practice-by-practice input from the projects. In the initial pilots, this approach proved very cumbersome. While very rigorous and with an excellent approach to corroboration, the method was not very efficient; appraisals took three long weeks, and the total effort expended by the appraised organization ran over 2,000 hours. This drove a new set of requirements for version 1.1 of the SCAMPI method, one of which was for an appraisal at maturity level 3 to take no more than 100 hours over 2 weeks for the on-site portion. While this was the stated requirement from the CMMI Steering Group, the team developing the method realized that it did not directly address the total time issue and that reducing on-site time by moving the same amount of work to the pre-on-site preparation phase did not achieve the real objective. As a result, the total impact on the appraised organization became the focus of the team. Pilots confirmed a 25 percent reduction in total time, with options available to reduce further. However, like gas mileage, your cost may vary depending on conditions and driving habits.

To a large extent, the length of the version 1.0 SCAMPI appraisals was due to the history of the method. When CBA-IPI was created, the organizations being assessed were generally quite immature. They were still learning what it meant to be level anything. Appraisals at maturity level 2 could not depend on the organization to provide an accurate evaluation. The CBA-IPI method, in application, assumed that the organization didn't know where they were. And, if they thought they did, they weren't to be believed. Documents are nice, but getting it from the horse's mouth (that is, the people who actually do the work) is

---

[1] Masters, S., and C. Bothwell, *CMM Appraisal Framework, Version 1.0 (CMU/SEI-95-TR-001)*. Pittsburgh, Software Engineering Institute, Carnegie Mellon University, February 1995.

better. In less mature organizations, the approach of getting practitioners in a room and letting them talk brings volumes of responses, and
with it increased confidence to the appraisal team that they have a sufficiently accurate understanding of the organization.

Many of these initial appraisals were at maturity level 2 and were limited to five or six process areas from the CMM for Software, depending
on whether subcontracting was included. At maturity level 3, there
were only 13 process areas. Also, the appraisals were limited to the software discipline, and the amount of data to be gathered was limited to
that part of the engineering organization. An approach that relied
heavily on interviews and on gathering observations from the notes
that the appraisal team members took during those interviews worked
in this environment. Observations could be collected, sorted, and analyzed without too much difficulty.

By the time that this approach was attempted with CMMI, three major
things had changed: The model had grown substantially, there were
multiple disciplines within the scope of an appraisal, and organizations being appraised were generally more mature. Not unlike the
CMM for Software, maturity level 2 in CMMI still has a small number
of process areas. However, CMMI maturity level 3 has 18, more if you
include within the appraisal scope the Integrated Product and Process
Development and Supplier Sourcing components. Within the software
discipline, maturity level 3 is often a minimum requirement and maturity level 5 is now not uncommon; and other disciplines are getting
involved and coming up to speed.

In an organization that is at maturity level 3, the working-level people
that are interviewed during an appraisal tend to talk not as much;
whereas a group at maturity level 1 or 2 has lots about which to com-
plain, a group at maturity level 3 knows what's going on and may give
the short answers. Consequently an appraisal team that relies primarily on notes from such interviews may not have the information it
needs. It helps if the team asks structured questions to force answers,
but this can become quite tedious if the session is expected to cover
everything. In contrast, basing the questions on the issues obtained
from evidence review can provide better coverage and focus.

As we will see in the discussion on SCAMPI planning later in this chapter (Section 3.3), a mature level 3 organization should know where they
stand before a SCAMPI is held. This is a basic premise of SCAMPI, one
that allows the major shift from the discovery approach of the CBA-IPI
method to verification, which we described earlier in Section 2.1.

Subtleties in the model architecture are additional drivers in the SCAMPI method. The CMM for Software has a loose relationship between practices and goals. There is a mapping in the appendix, but practices in the CMM for Software often map to more than one goal. This is due to some compound requirements in the practice statements. In contrast, the structure of EIA 731 tied practices uniquely to "themes," which in the 731 model are roughly equivalent to goals in CMMI. The integrated CMMI models follow the EIA-731 approach by breaking up such practice statements and making each practice align with exactly one goal. This allows a more structured scoring and rating logic, based upon a more structured approach to the evidence review and the ability to have a clearer picture of the status before going into interviews.

Another feature of SCAMPI is its detailed *Method Description Document* (MDD), something that was lacking with the CBA-IPI method. This document addresses what we call here the SCAMPI Class A Method Definition. The SCAMPI method version 1.1 provides a comprehensive, publicly available definition of the appraisal process. It clearly articulates what is required, what the allowable tailoring options are, and what is just guidance. These are in the sections of the MDD on Required Practices, Parameters and Limits, Optional Practices, and Implementation Guidance. Another change is the recognition that the SCAMPI MDD is the rulebook. In the past, changes to the CBA-IPI method were introduced by means of changes to the training provided to lead assessors. Changes to SCAMPI must be made by means of changes to the MDD, through the public and controlled CMMI change approval process.

Included in the tailoring options for SCAMPI are adjustments to the method for when a SCAMPI is conducted for an external appraisal, particularly in a source selection environment. These options came from the *Software Capability Evaluation* (SCE) method, which is used with the CMM for Software, and reflect the realities of evaluating multiple bidders in a competitive legal environment.[2] The adjustments are evident in the two nominal schedules that we provide in Chapter 5, "SCAMPI for Internal Process Improvement," and Chapter 6, "SCAMPI for External Audits."

---

[2] Byrnes, P., and M. Phillips, *Software Capability Evaluation Version 3.0 Method Description (CMU/SEI-96-TR-002)*. Pittsburgh, Software Engineering Institute, Carnegie Mellon University, April 1996.

3.2 SCAMPI PIIDs

The changes in SCAMPI tied to verification have one key concept that is both useful and risky to the organization and the appraisal. That concept is *Process Implementation Indicators* (PIIs) and *Process Implementation Indicator Descriptions* (PIIDs). They are useful in that they can identify the available artifacts of process implementation; they are risky in that they can lead to a "checklist mentality."

The basic concept of a PIID that is of most value is as a vehicle to maintain awareness of how process implementation is progressing on projects and within the organization overall.[3] By maintaining some record of the resulting products of process use and where to find the most important ones, the organization monitors actual usage. When this is coupled with the product and process monitoring and measurement processes, the process group can maintain a fairly clear picture of what's really happening.

In preparing for a SCAMPI, this knowledge makes the lead appraiser's life considerably easier. Because the organization can show which projects are doing what, what evidence exists, and where the evidence is, the lead can more easily see the overall organizational picture. Selecting projects to address development life-cycle coverage and specific artifacts to review becomes a selection task rather than a "bring me a rock" exercise.

The lead appraiser can see where new processes may have implementation risks, in that artifacts from projects starting to use the new processes are not available. If the process group is aware of the status and can identify the times that the processes will produce evidence, the lead appraiser and the organization can make much better judgments on scheduling the appraisal.

Sample PIIDs are provided in Appendix B, "Practice Implementation Indicator Descriptions," for the purpose of providing examples of typical artifacts that may be used as evidence for individual practices. The use of PIIDs is covered in more detail in Section 7.2. Each organization needs to identify the appropriate products for their processes. The projects will then have to tailor these concepts for their own situation.

---

[3] In the CMMI Model, a specific practice in the Organizational Process Focus (OPF) process area deals with implementing process action plans (SP 2.2). PIIDs can be useful in tracking progress against such a plan.

Also, the lead appraiser may have preferences on which products most accurately reflect implementation in a specific instance.

The downside of PIIDs is that they can become a checklist. They can lead to the expectation that the typical work products listed in the models are mandatory, which without question they are not. It is with this caution that we provide the sample PIIDs.

3.3 Preparation—Before Going Off to the Races

Conducting a SCAMPI appraisal is a complex operation, and the SCAMPI method places considerable emphasis on thorough planning and on timely and effective preparation for the appraisal. Figure 3-1 shows the *Plan and Prepare for Appraisals Processes* identified in the MDD. The MDD provides a listing of activities for each of the steps shown in the flow.

Successful execution of the SCAMPI plan depends on having a well-qualified and trained team, and on having the material and logistic support items ready. During the planning and preparation phase the appraisal team reviews the knowledge of and presence of objective evidence that is critical for a verification approach rather than a discovery approach. These things will not happen by accident, making the preparation phase critical to success.

The planning and preparation phase of Figure 3-1 has two important inputs. The first is the general requirements for the appraisal. The requirements (and constraints) are needed to kick off the Analyze Requirements process that begins with identifying the appraisal objectives. The second is the initial objective evidence, which also affects the definition of the appraisal objectives.

3.3.1 Why Are We Doing This?

The objectives developed in the *Analyze Requirements* phase must answer this question. The answers will vary from organization to organization, but in general there are three modes of usage identified in SCAMPI. They are internal process improvement, supplier selection, and process monitoring. While CMMI was not written with much consideration given to its use as a source selection tool, the authors recognized that probably it would be used in that manner. The inclusion of external appraisals in SCAMPI is in recognition of this fact of life.

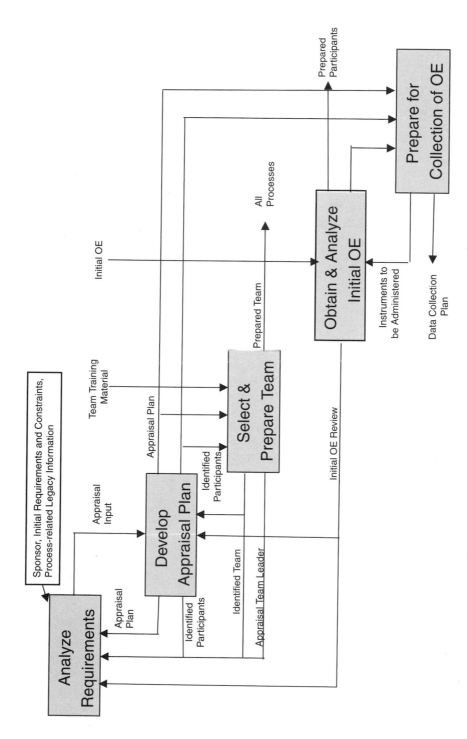

Figure 3-1: *Plan and Prepare for Appraisals—Process Flow*

The purpose of an organization's internal SCAMPI should be to evaluate how process improvement is going and what the next steps should be. However, getting a number to fill a square is sometimes the real purpose. An organization that has clear business objectives for improved performance is more likely to be at the "process improvement" end of the spectrum. The appraisal team should expect a more difficult appraisal as the mode shifts to the "get a number" end of the spectrum.

The other usage modes are source selection or process monitoring. A source selection appraisal can be internal or external and can have a process improvement or "get a number" flavor. Quite often, an acquirer may establish a requirement for suppliers to meet a number in order to submit a competitive bid. This runs the risk of directing the focus away from the real benefit of process improvement and may be counterproductive in the long run. One effective way to use the CMMI and SCAMPI for source selection and still retain the process improvement-focus is to request a gap or risk analysis, which identifies shortfalls and defines improvements to fix them. The scope of the appraisal can be a specified maturity level or a set of process areas that are of particular concern to the customer for the project. This approach can also be used during a contract to monitor the progress of an organization's process improvement.

It must be noted that the SCAMPI Class A appraisal method is quite rigorous and can be expensive to apply. In pilots, the lower end of effort was 1,500 hours to prepare and conduct a maturity level 3 SCAMPI. This lower-end number was for very mature organizations that were fully aware of their status and well into the verification mode. As maturity diminishes, the effort goes up. The SCAMPI authors understood this and recognized that organizations that are not at least at maturity level 3 will encounter difficulties. One mitigating factor is that a maturity level 2 SCAMPI has a much smaller number of process areas to address. However, unless a formal rating is required, in order to reduce the appraisal expenditure we would recommend that less mature organizations use Class B or C appraisals or internal methods to establish the initial state or to measure progress.

The first step in defining the objectives is to identify and establish communications between the sponsor and the relevant stakeholders. At least one interaction between the lead appraiser and the sponsor is required, and together they should be sure to determine the stated and unstated reasons for the appraisal.

Besides the lead appraiser and the sponsor, another essential relevant stakeholder is the site coordinator, who will lead the effort for the appraised organization. This is the person who leads planning, directs internal preparations, suggests team members (if internal), arranges logistics, and generally implements the appraisal. The more familiar this person is with the model and the method, the better. However, knowledge of the organization and where it is in the process improvement program is essential. The lead appraiser can make up for shortcomings in the first area, but not the second.

3.3.1.1 Model Scope

The two principal dimensions of appraisal scope are model and organization. The first question is how much of the model will be used in the appraisal. The second is the size of the organization. These two parameters are major contributors to the effort involved in the appraisal.

The basic decisions on model scope include how many of the process areas will be appraised and to what level. These factors are related to whether a single-number maturity level or an individual capability level rating on each process area is desired.

For each maturity level, the CMMI prescribes a defined set of process areas and how the generic goals will be applied. The only significant variation in scope would be for maturity levels 4 and 5. For these levels, the subprocesses that are quantitatively managed must be defined and do not have to include the entire set.

For capability levels, the process areas appraised can be any subset of the model.[4] Further, the levels appraised can be totally independent of each other. The result can be a much more varied profile, as shown in Figure 3-2. Capability levels provide the opportunity to look at some process areas that are quite mature and at the same time give an appropriate appraisal of process areas that may be just starting out. This approach provides more flexibility to focus on specific business needs. An organization that specializes in development or testing of requirements can put emphasis on their most critical processes.

Regardless of which path is chosen, avoid the temptation to enter into long debates about whether to use the staged or continuous representations;

---

[4] The wise use of a continuous model requires a clear understanding of the many inherent ordering relationships between various model elements. There are many subsets of the model that would constitute a poor choice upon which to base an appraisal. The lead appraiser can assist an organization in understanding these relationships.

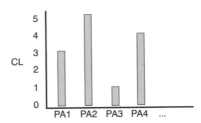

Figure 3-2: *Process Area Capability Levels*

there is only one CMMI. The requirements of the two representations are identical. In the continuous representation of the CMMI models, Appendix F on *Equivalent Staging* provides the rules for using the material in that representation to provide maturity level ratings.[5]

There have been appraisals that provide both maturity and capability levels. If the scope is a straight maturity level 2 or 3 and the target levels are achieved, this is both simple and redundant. However, if the target is not met, particularly in a level 3 (or above) appraisal, it can be valuable to record partial credit. If one practice is not implemented, it can drop the maturity level rating back to level 2 or even 1. The same results could also be presented as capability level 3 in 17 process areas and 2 (or lower) in the one problem process area.

One other area of potential confusion between maturity and capability is what happens at levels 4 and 5. It stems in part from the historical use of capability levels in source models that did not provide a single number, but users still wanted to target and advertise single numbers. In these situations, it became common practice to aim for a single level for all process areas appraised. This worked well at levels up to level 3 and did not differ significantly from the maturity level approach. However, at level 4 or 5 this assumption requires significantly more coverage than for maturity levels. This was specifically resolved in the Equivalent Staging approach, and the two are now identical.

3.3.1.2 Organization Scope

The definition of the organization to be appraised frequently has been a complex challenge. As we noted before, the organization can cover an entire company, a business unit, parts of the company with a similar need, a single project, a group of projects, or almost any combination that one can dream up. These options alone make for tough decisions.

---

[5] Some refer to this (tongue in cheek) as the "constaguous" approach.

In the past, the organization was usually restricted to either software developers or systems engineers. CMMI brings (and therefore SCAMPI faces) additional challenges of multiple disciplines.

In the case of a software-only appraisal, it has been a relatively easy and fairly common practice to isolate the group of interest in its own world of process maturity. A software group can have its own plan, training program, quality group, configuration management, and so on. A relatively clear boundary could be drawn for the appraisal, and the team knows where to look for evidence.

For systems engineering, there is a broader scope and the boundaries are fuzzier. There is usually a Systems Engineering Management Plan, but the scope is closer to the overall program plan and the responsibilities of program management. There is seldom a separate quality or configuration management function. The appraiser makes more use of this approach: "I don't care who does it, does it get done?"

CMMI now provides the basis for SCAMPI appraisals of both software and systems engineering at the same time. However, neither the model nor the appraisal method provides the specifics in how to plan and conduct such an appraisal. This becomes even more important when the full power of CMMI is applied and additional disciplines, from hardware or program management to the entire company, are added. Several options are available and have been applied. Let's first address just the systems and software case.

The first and most straightforward approach is to have two separate appraisals. There can be some overlap in planning and preparations, but this basically means twice the effort of a single SCAMPI. Further, it defeats the basic premise of CMMI, which is meant to encourage the integration of processes. A rule of thumb is that if the organization has separate processes for each discipline, there will be two appraisals to cover the two disciplines. However, if the disciplines' processes are integrated, a single set of objective evidence will cover both disciplines: a single appraisal.[6]

A variation on this approach is to have a single appraisal with separate ratings for the disciplines. The execution isn't much different because the appraisers still have to fulfill the evidence requirements for both disciplines. Fortunately some common process areas (such as the organizational ones) apply to both disciplines, which reduces the workload.

---

[6] Alas, often the reality is that some are integrated and some are separate.

However, that may be negated by the effort to keep the two sets of books straight for the other process areas.

The approach that most directly supports the intent of the CMMI is a combined appraisal with one rating. There may still be different artifacts for each discipline, such as a Systems Engineering Master Plan (SEMP) and a Software Development Plan (SDP). However, this approach allows systems engineering to be responsible for translating customer needs into requirements (see Requirements Development, Specific Goal 1) and software to have increased involvement in the derivation of requirements (see RD, SG 2). It also adds impetus to using a single configuration management process with tailored procedures for hardware and software, a single quality process, and an integrated organizational training effort.

In many cases, the organization may prefer the approach of a combined appraisal with one rating but is facing the fact that software is operating at a different (today, typically higher) maturity level than systems engineering. If the difference is level 3 versus 2 or lower, one of the first two approaches—separate appraisals or separate scores—may be best. If the difference is software at level 4 or 5 and systems engineering at level 3, this can be handled without going all the way back to one of the first two approaches. A combined appraisal can address all requirements up through level 3, and the level 4 or 5 activities of software can be looked at separately.

3.3.2 Things to Look Out For

For every appraisal there are constraints within which the team must operate, and there are risks that must be managed.

3.3.2.1 Constraints

As much as the lead appraiser may want to have total control of the appraisal, appraisals must still be conducted in the real world. Organizations usually have some set of drivers that affect the appraisal. These might be external constraints such as a need to be ready for a proposal or meet a contract requirement, or they might be created internally. Internal targets are good for pushing process improvement. However, when they become part of management incentives they develop a life of their own.

The appraisal team may have to work around the program schedules. The week of a major program review or deployment event is not a good time for an appraisal. Classified programs may limit access to data. Selection of team members with access can resolve this, but the plan must take into account that the data will not be freely available for establishing team consensus.

Other constraints include holidays, culture, and work agreements. In France, there are restrictions on overtime. An appraisal in New Orleans during Mardi Gras may sound like fun (and surely it would be), but it is not practical.

3.3.2.2 Risks

SCAMPI requires that the risks associated with the appraisal be identified and mitigated. Also, key risks must have mitigations planned and executed. The sponsor is to be kept informed about the status of the risks and mitigation actions.

There are several categories of risk associated with the conduct of the appraisal itself. Particularly for a lower-maturity organization that is in a discovery mode, the ability to gather the needed artifacts will be a higher risk. If the team is less experienced, there is a risk that the efficiency of the appraisal will suffer. When using electronic data sources, the links are at risk of not working. Each of these can be dealt with in the planning and preparation for the appraisal.

Unfortunately there is a real risk related to interpretations of the model. The initial application of CMMI to an organization runs into problems with interpreting the intended meaning of the model. Another issue is application of the model in a new context where the practices may not apply as originally conceived. Using early Class B and C appraisals to work out such issues with the SCAMPI team members and lead can be very effective. If serious interpretation issues arise, don't hesitate to ask the SEI directly for a clarification either by phone or email, or through www.sei.cmu.edu.

Another risk that should be addressed is the risk to and within the organization if the results are not those expected. Hopefully, those involved have reasonable expectations and see the appraisal as a measure of progress. However, there are situations where sponsors view the appraisal a pass/fail situation or the impact of an appraisal is significant. The first line of mitigation for these situations is preparation with good internal knowledge of the status before starting a SCAMPI, including appropriate Class B or C appraisals. In the planning phase, extra care should be taken in defining the artifacts needed and in a

Readiness Review (see Section 3.3.7). During the appraisal, all negative findings that may impact the ratings must be carefully documented.

3.3.3 Putting It on the Record

It will come as no surprise that there are a lot of decisions and arrangements to be made in preparation for a SCAMPI appraisal. Many of them are critical to success. To avoid either misunderstanding of a key point or missing a decision, an approved plan is a mandatory output of the *Develop Appraisal Plan* phase; it is required prior to starting the appraisal. The decisions on objectives, scope, and outputs that are documented in the *Appraisal Input* are the heart of the plan. There are other components to the plan, such as logistics, that will have a large effect on the overall conduct and effectiveness of the appraisal.

3.3.3.1 Visiting the SCAMPI Tailor

Each of the activities of SCAMPI has a range of application and identification of optional practices. These decisions must be made to define the conduct of the appraisal. Some of the options are

- Inclusion of presentations or demonstrations, particularly tools, as objective evidence
- Requests for interviewees to bring a document to the interview
- Use of video/teleconference for interviews
- Instantiation-level decisions by mini-team or full team
- Reporting of findings by project
- Including ratings in the final presentation

While some of these may be subject to circumstance, they need to be discussed in the plan as acceptable or not. An example is the use of teleconference interviews if the possibility has been identified that someone may be out of town. The plan should state whether the teleconference is acceptable or whether a different person needs to be interviewed.

3.3.3.2 What Do You Get for Your Money?

Failure to address this question specifically can cause much consternation at the end of the appraisal during the *Report Results* phase (see Figure 3-3). There are mandatory outputs that include the Appraisal Record, Appraisal Disclosure Statement, and Appraisal Report. The appraisal also results in goal ratings for all goals within the scope. At a minimum these will be provided to the sponsor, as well as any final findings, including strengths and weaknesses.

Beyond that, there are several optional outputs, including the maturity or capability level ratings and the discipline-specific or project-specific ratings. The sponsor and lead appraiser should specifically address the risks and possible situations that might cause the sponsor to suddenly desire a different output halfway through the appraisal.

For more detailed results, practice-level characterizations can be requested. In some cases, an organization may wish project-specific findings or ratings. These are not recommended unless special circumstances are present. The practice-level characterizations are generally far too detailed to be useful in a presentation or report. If there is a particular practice that needs attention, it should be addressed in a finding against the process area. In fact, even a subpractice can cause a finding.

Project-specific findings place the confidentiality of the appraisal in jeopardy and influence the openness of interviews. In any case, problems that rise to the level of a finding at level 3 and above are generally across multiple projects and need to be addressed as an organizational issue. Should there need to be actions taken that need to address specific projects, the local team members can help provide focus.

A formal Final Report is not mandatory, but may be provided. In many cases, the final briefing is the only documentation provided in addition to the mandatory reports. It might be valuable to have the appraisal team document at least some explanations of the findings to be sure their real meaning isn't forgotten shortly after the team leaves. Appraisal activities may also extend into action planning. This should be considered as additional to the intended scope of SCAMPI, but can be a way to take advantage of the experience of a talented appraisal team.

Other optional outputs include the team's estimation of the consequences of what they observed, together with recommendations. It can be very beneficial to take advantage of the team's expertise in this fashion. It is particularly helpful when team members from outside the organization can give fresh views on problems to the organization.

3.3.3.3 And the Essential Basics

Those experienced in appraisals are not surprised by the amount of resources involved, but first-timers usually are. Even an experienced person needs to take care not to miss key elements. SCAMPI includes three related activities covering resources, cost, schedule, and overall logistics.

The scope of the appraisal determines who will be participating, and when. While the lead appraiser will be concerned first about the representative sample of projects included in the appraisal, the project schedules must be taken into consideration. It's difficult to get the full attention of a project manager if the appraisal occurs simultaneously with a major review, test, or deployment.

The appraisal team should be the largest component in estimating the resources, provided that the organization is prepared for a full verification mode appraisal. When the appraisal team must go into a discovery mode and dig for artifacts, not only will the appraisal length be expanded but also the preparation time may well double.

The requirement for a detailed cost estimate touches on some sensitive subjects. Most organizations are not eager to release the information associated with rates that would be necessary for costing. The effort does need to be defined in the plan and the costs known for internal budgeting.

Due to the volume of information in a SCAMPI, tools are practically required. Also, the use of computer projectors is advised for all team-wide consensus activities. It's a lot more efficient to reach agreement on meaning or wording when everyone is viewing the same data.

The SCAMPI MDD provides a good list of logistic concerns, down to the level of hotel accommodations for out-of-town participants and food for the team members. However, the issue of escorts needs more emphasis. To whatever extent is possible, the team, and particularly the lead appraiser, should have access without escorts, as well as appropriate security clearances to access all relevant data. This is beneficial for some mini-team activities and the general ability of the team to function effectively.

3.3.4 Getting the Team Together

As much as the CMMI authors worked to reduce the variation of interpretations that can be given to the model, there is still room for discussion and debate in a particular situation. This lends a special importance to the *Select and Prepare Team* phase. The lead appraiser does not need to understand your business in depth, but he or she must have the understanding of the model to be able to adapt it to new situations.

Another concern for choosing among lead appraisers should be their interpretations of broad areas, such as what is required for institution-alization. Some lead appraisers that are used to short-duration soft-ware projects are slow to adapt to the realities of longer development life cycles at the systems level. In general, the lead appraiser needs to understand where their background is lacking and assure that the team composition covers any gaps. In some teams, a second or assistant lead has been used to provide expertise complementary to the official lead.

Even though the SEI runs a very comprehensive program to assure the quality of Authorized Lead Appraisers, situations occasionally arise where a lead appears to be giving an overly strict interpretation of the model. Examples include requiring Direct and Indirect artifacts for each practice, requiring evidence for subpractices, or insisting on see-ing all typical work products. One possible solution is to ask for a sec-ond opinion from a different appraiser. In any case, do not hesitate to ask the SEI directly for a clarification as discussed under risks. This is one method of feedback that helps ensure a higher-quality appraisal system.

The team needs to have broad and deep experience in the subjects addressed. In a full maturity level 3 appraisal, it helps to have members with a broad background so the team is not relying on the sole expert in several areas. In multidomain appraisals, such as an SE/SW appraisal, the team must have full coverage of the domains to be appraised.

In general, it's easier to take a subject matter expert and help them with the model and method requirements than to take a model expert and help them apply it to a specific area, such as configuration manage-ment. Do not rely too heavily on the minimum required training in doing this. Basic education theory tells you that the student will retain less than 20% of the information and begin to forget that in a relatively short period of time. If the option is taken to provide training to a large group of future team members, this retention issue needs to be remem-bered unless the delay is very short. Also, the training does a good job of introducing the basics but is not able to cover the depth of under-standing required for some of the more difficult decisions that may arise.

To mitigate the risks involved with this problem, the lead appraiser needs to ensure the team members are properly interpreting the model as the appraisal progresses. This is one reason that the lead appraiser should not be a mini-team member except in the smallest appraisals. Another mitigation is to combine the method training with the Readiness Review and use actual artifacts in the training session. It's a good idea to use the tailoring option of doing the method training "just-in-time" as the appraisal progresses.

3.3.5 Getting the Evidence

This is where the lead appraiser determines how difficult the appraisal will be and how much discovery will be needed. An organization that truly knows where they are starts out with a good mapping of the model to the internal processes, accurate awareness of which processes are being applied where, and knowledge of what artifacts are being generated and where they are located. This is covered in the *Obtain and Analyze Initial Objective Evidence* phase. In actuality, if an organization is well prepared, the team will be able to conduct a verification of that knowledge, and planning is relatively easy. However, where this is not the case, there will be a long period of understanding the evidence needs and finding the artifacts. This is why the SCAMPI method shows an output from this activity back as an input to *Analyze Requirements* and *Develop Appraisal Plan* (see Figure 3-1).

One of the most discussed aspects of this and following activities dealing with artifacts is the distinction between direct and indirect artifacts. If you paint the house, a painted house is a *direct* artifact. Receipts for the paint or empty cans are *indirect*, as is a note from a spouse that compliments the job. Some artifacts may serve both purposes for different practices. For instance, peer review minutes may be a direct artifact of the review and indirect for the item under review. Likewise, direct evidence of monitoring is also indirect evidence of planning.

Another source of evidence is the instrument, which is a part of the *Prepare for Collection of Objective Evidence* phase. Several forms have been used, from general questions about the state of practice, to detailed questionnaires asking about individual practices. Yes-or-no questions have limited value. Questionnaire responses that briefly address how the practice is performed and put the evidence provided in context are very useful to the appraisal team. Remember that the PIIDs list is an instrument, too. Explanatory notes in a PIID that explain the context and meaning of the evidence presented are both informative and can be used as affirmations.

The instrument is one place that the SCAMPI can be tailored for the maturity of the organization. In lower-maturity organizations, a questionnaire addressing the specific practices can provide useful information. For a level 4 or 5 organization, such questions are of limited value; however, questions addressing the actual use of quantitative data would be appropriate and informative.

Preliminary activities including Class B and C appraisals are also good sources of evidence. While some of the evidence in a preliminary appraisal may grow stale, it is a lot easier to review and replace as necessary than to start with a blank page.

In any case, those involved with providing evidence, before or during the appraisal, need to be informed about what's going on and their part in it. They should not need to be model experts. The language of the model and the instrument should be tailored to local phraseology wherever possible. It is helpful to educate participants on how the appraisal will be conducted and the general concepts of maturity. Hopefully, they will have experienced the correct application on the job. What should be avoided is difficulty expressing that fact due to language differences.

One way to help this is to have a short class on the model just before administering any instrument and possibly having someone available to answer questions as it's being completed. This occurs more frequently at lower levels.

The details of what will be collected, who will be interviewed, and who will review what information and in what manner will be the final product of the planning effort. This is also the one part of the planning that should be updated as the appraisal progresses, for during that time the appraisal team may identify additional artifacts that it needs. Typically, the item requested is not what was expected or raises some issue that additional evidence can resolve. Besides artifacts, additional interviews can be requested to resolve these issues or some arising from the interview process. The more favorable occurrence is to cancel an interview because all information anticipated is already available.

3.3.6 The Patchwork Quilt Issue

One problem faced in implementing the CMMI is that many organizations have program life cycles that are longer than the process improvement and appraisal cycle. On the one hand, it is now common to have projects that have been ongoing for many years as candidates for appraisal. For projects that are implementing new processes near the end of their life, it doesn't make sense to go back and redo the front end planning or requirements just for appraisal purposes. On the other hand, those projects that are using the current processes for front-end activities will have little, if any, evidence beyond initial planning for verification and product integration.

In recognition of this, SCAMPI does not require that a single project provide full coverage of the development life cycle. To respond to this challenge, the organization needs to understand and communicate to the lead appraiser the details of process implementation within the projects. Several organizations have been able to map their internal practices to process areas of the model and show which projects have been grandfathered out of recently introduced early-phase practices, which have used legacy processes, which have not yet performed later-phase practices, and when they are planned to be done.

With this knowledge, the lead appraiser can more confidently address life-cycle coverage along with the other concerns in selecting the projects to be reviewed as part of the appraisal. It also allows inclusion of new-start projects to see how the future is progressing without their lack of progress deep into the life cycle being an issue.

Where possible, projects should be appraised for the entire development life cycle to see the continuity of the overall process. Also, extreme use of this approach may give the appearance of cherry-picking the best examples. To keep the confusion and negative impressions to a minimum, this approach should be limited to where it is truly needed.

3.3.7 Are We Ready?

The Readiness Review is the final decision point that it's time to gather the team and proceed with the appraisal. At least one Readiness Review is required, but more may be needed. This is particularly true in a first try. It's not mandatory that everything be in place at the review, just that there is reasonable confidence that any holes will be filled before the start. It is also not the intent that this be a full appraisal-level review of the evidence. The evidence should be reviewed for coverage and general correctness.

While the Readiness Review can be performed by the lead appraiser, it has also been found effective to combine it with team training and use the whole team.

One last review that a lead appraiser should make is to look at the feasibility of the appraisal plan. With everything that is in place, are the risks mitigated and is the appraisal likely to achieve its objectives? If too much data is missing, too many actions are still open, time constraints are too tight, or other serious problems exist, now is the time to consider rescheduling or adding resources. In any case, the sponsor must be made aware of the risk status.

Now that the planning has been completed and the organization is ready, it's time to start the real appraisal.

On your mark, get set . . .

3.4 Conducting an Appraisal

When everything is in place, it's time to actually conduct the appraisal. Figure 3-3 shows the *Conduct Appraisal Processes Flow*. The MDD lists activities for each process step. The processes cover a lot of information and can be time consuming. The preparation phase has been designed to maximize effectiveness and efficiency. There are also features of the actual on-site conduct that will help to minimize the pain. Depending on the scope of the appraisal, there are a specific number of small and large decisions to make. SCAMPI is designed to allow the lead appraiser to track these decisions to closure and manage the appraisal.

A critical component of an effective and efficient appraisal is the concept of focused investigation. During the development of SCAMPI, the term "triage" was used, which means a "sorting." Although that term does not appear in the MDD, it does convey the idea. The team must decide those things that are obvious, either good or bad, and apply their focus to those decisions that need more attention. This is intended to produce both a more accurate result and minimize the time spent on achieving it.

For instance, suppose that all projects provide strong evidence of risk management through plans, reports, tool demonstrations, risk charts in management reviews, training records, and other evidence. At the same time, there is little guidance on decision processes, trade studies have weak definition of criteria or inconclusive decisions, and several generic practices have questionable evidence. The appraisal team should focus their activities more on resolving the extent of practice for *Decision Analysis and Resolution* (DAR) rather than *Risk Management*

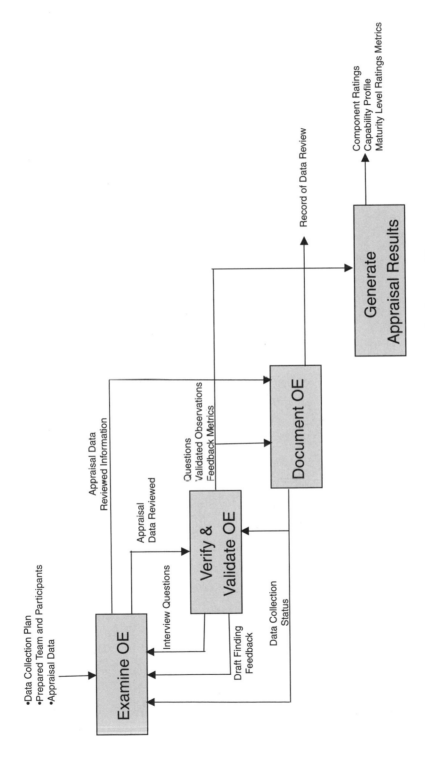

Figure 3-3: *Conduct Appraisal—Process Flow*

(RSKM). This is particularly true with the number and priority of the interview questions. This is not a new idea; it's just new to being explicitly part of an appraisal method.

Before starting, we provide a word of caution. The idea circulates from time to time that an organization can proceed into the appraisal and, after determining how the evidence plays out, decide if it's a SCAMPI A or a Class B appraisal. Such may not be the case if the decision is made after the Final Findings are presented. Aborting a SCAMPI A is one thing, and the MDD does not address specifics on how to do that. To be a SCAMPI A, the preliminary work must have been completed as well as the actual appraisal steps. The best way to proceed is to start with the SCAMPI preparation activities first. The best time to make the go or no-go decision is at the Readiness Review.

3.4.1 Examining and Verifying the Evidence

As a result of the Readiness Review, the presence of evidence should be known. Now the team enters in earnest into the *Examine Objective Evidence* and *Verify and Validate Objective Evidence* phases. Some holes may have been identified and the risk deemed acceptable. However, in most cases, the team will be aware that sufficient evidence is available to answer the questions. What isn't known is whether the evidence will answer the question adequately, or provide strengths or weaknesses.

For example, trade studies presented for evidence of the practices in DAR might be missing the identification of decision criteria. Or, they might identify a strength in the variety of methods applied. Granted, a Readiness Review may uncover the lack of criteria in the trade studies proposed. However, if the review is going to the level of whether the variety of methods applied is a strength, it's overdoing it.

3.4.1.1 How Much Is Enough

Before jumping into actually looking at the evidence, it pays to remember how much and what types are required. For this we need to address direct and indirect artifacts and affirmations. These were described in Chapter 2, "New Aspects of the SCAMPI Method," with the exception of interviews. In this section, we will discuss how they are applied during the appraisal.

For starters, SCAMPI requires one direct artifact for each instance of a practice being performed on an appraised project. A direct artifact is something that would be a direct result of the effort.[7] For defining requirements, the direct artifact would be the requirements in some form, which could be a specification document or a computer-based requirements database. Paper is not required. However, the team must be able to take a look at some form of product.

An additional form of evidence must support the direct evidence. One type of evidence that could be used in support of the direct evidence is an indirect artifact. This is, anything that provides evidence of a direct artifact but is not the direct artifact itself. For the requirements example, minutes of a requirements review or a work breakdown task referencing the requirements indicate their existence but are not the requirements themselves.

For some reason, the distinction between direct and indirect causes difficulties for many appraisal participants. Patient discussions with the lead appraiser should resolve questions.

Presentations may be used during a SCAMPI, for example tool demonstrations, or tours of the Process Asset Library. A good use of presentations is to familiarize the team with the organization and projects that will be the subject of the appraisal. In this case, they should be done early so that the team will have the context for the document reviews. Presentations can also be very effective for topics such as quantitative management at level 4 and 5. When the people who use the measurements describe what they are and how they use them live, the team gets an understanding that is not achievable by other means.

Another excellent application of presentations occurs when a process is embodied in a tool. Configuration management and risk management are examples of where this may apply. A session with the tool user is considerably more informative and easier to put together than generating and explaining screenshots, data dumps, and reports.

Some practices are less amenable to direct evidence. For instance, commitment can be recorded on a signature sheet, but does that really show the intent of the signatory? A policy statement is easy to produce but making the content actually be the policy in the organization is more difficult to accomplish and to confirm. For these, other means must be used to make a confident determination.

---

[7] For a practice, direct artifacts from more than one project or program may be needed to show that the use of the practice is widespread and "institutionalized."

Regarding interviews, a valuable tool in appraisals is face-to-face contact. Yes, people can be coached and will tend to be careful with their answers. However, the interview continues to reveal significant insight as to what is really going on.

Interviews are affected by the maturity of the organization, particularly practitioner groups. The original theory was that the group assembled and was asked to discuss how they conducted development. After over an hour of letting off steam, the team would have to bring things to an end and send them on their way. The practitioners had plenty to say. This was also characteristic of the discovery mode of appraisal.

As organizations got closer to level 3, things quieted down. Some might say it was due to being coached. A more consistent explanation is that the interviewees knew their processes had a straightforward answer. At this point, the team needed to have more specific questions to raise. Improved document reviews provided this information. The interviews became more focused on the issues at hand. It is this environment that SCAMPI addresses, and the document reviews are intended to prepare the team to focus on the right issues.

As maturity increased further, the trend reversed. Interviewees now not only knew they had the answer, but they had the measures to prove it. And, the team was not getting away without hearing the full story. The appraisal team should be prepared for that to occur.

One way the team can improve interviews is by assuring that some members of the team are included for their interpersonal skills. Using people to lead sessions with whom the interview participants are comfortable is beneficial.

A caution on technology: We are now getting to the point that some team members are more comfortable taking notes on laptops. This can be beneficial in having a record of the sessions later. It can also be very distracting to have what looks and sounds like a row of court reporters clicking away while someone is trying to answer a question. A compromise is to have one or two keyboarders and have the rest of the team write manually.

3.4.1.2 There Is a Minimum

In all likelihood the review of documents will provide at least two sources of implementation evidence for each practice as implemented on each project (as applicable). The method requires this coverage to clearly demonstrate that the practices claimed are actually occurring. However, the SCAMPI authors were concerned that the appraisal could turn into simply a document review of direct and indirect artifacts. To prevent this, the MDD (2.2.1) contains a requirement for face-to-face affirmations:

> *Obtain face-to-face affirmations corresponding to each specific and generic goal within the model scope of the appraisal for either (1) at least one instantiation for every associated practice and at least one practice for every associated instantiation for the goal (i.e., 1-row, 1-column) or (2) at least 50% of the cells corresponding to the instantiation/practice matrix for the goal.*

This does not mean that a separate question is needed for each practice nor that separate questions be addressed to each program in group interviews. It does mean that the team needs to pay attention to the answers and the discussion in order to address as many practices as possible and credit all responding programs in group interviews.

While the minimum requirement does avoid one risk, it raises another. If not careful, the team can turn the interviews into a box-filling exercise. One of the advantages of the triage approach is to be able to focus the interviews on the areas that need discussion. It would be a shame to lose this benefit in the headlong rush to check boxes.

3.4.1.3 Checking the Library—Objective Evidence Review

The requirement is for one direct artifact per practice. Sometimes more than one is needed to fully determine implementation. Also, some practices have compound requirements that may not be covered by a single artifact. For instance, the first Specific Practice in Risk Management calls for determining risk sources and categories. This might require two direct artifacts, the first describing risk sources and the second describing risk categories.

On the other hand, a single artifact often serves several purposes. A trade study can cover most of Decision Analysis and Resolution while also addressing several practices in Technical Solutions. An engineering change will be direct evidence of configuration management and may also be direct evidence of requirements analysis. A training record for generic practices in a given process area may also be direct evidence of monitoring and controlling the organizational training.

Remember that PIIDs are instruments, and inputs such as feedback on preliminary findings may be considered a presentation.

As the evidence review begins, so does the tracking to closure and the application of focused investigation or "triage." Because the number of practice decisions is known, the team can monitor how many have evidence to make them and how many are still open. Most of the decisions should be reached fairly easily. If the initial answer, at least as far as documented evidence goes, is clearly yes or no, the team should note that and press on. There will be several areas where the evidence presented leaves the answer uncertain. This is where attention should be paid.

3.4.2 Documenting Evidence and Generating Results

Options to resolve ambiguities include requests for additional artifacts and questions to be asked in the interviews. In theory, the Readiness Review should have provided enough evidence to determine practice implementation. However, when the evidence is reviewed in detail, sometimes the artifact is inadequate in some way. For instance, a project plan may end up not completely addressing data management as anticipated and a request may be for a referenced document to answer the issue. When additional evidence is needed, the team (as part of the *Document Objective Evidence* phase) re-plans the Data Collection Plan as provided for in SCAMPI.

Several methods can be used during the *Document Objective Evidence* phase to evaluate the adequacy of the documents for the practices. Two examples are shown here for consideration.

The following document is used to show how the GPs have been "planned."[8]

---

[8] These charts are used with permission from Cooliemon, LLC.

Document/Section

Generic Practice	ReqM	PP	PMC	SAM	MA	PPQA	CM
GP2.2—Plan the Process	PMP 4.1	Plan Matrix, Entry Criteria	PMP 4.1 PMP 5	PMP 4.1	PMP 4.1 PMP 5.4	PMP 4.1 PMP 4.5.2	PMP 4.1 PMP 4.5.1 PMP 4.5.2
GP2.3—Provide Resources	PMP 3	Plan Matrix, Entry Criteria	PMP 3	PMP 3	PMP 3	PMP 3	PMP 3
GP2.4—Assign Responsibility	PMP 3.1.7	Plan Matrix, Entry Criteria	PMP 3.1.4	PMP 3.1.4	PMP 3.1.4	PMP 3.1.6	PMP 3.1.8
GP2.5—Train People	PMP 3.3	Plan Matrix, Entry Criteria	PMP 3.3	PMP 3.3	PMP 3.3	PMP 3.3	PMP 3.3
GP2.6—Manage Configurations	PMP 2.4	Plan Matrix, Entry Criteria	PMP 2.4	PMP 2.4	PMP 2.4	PMP 2.4	PMP 2.4
GP2.7—Identify and Involve Relevant Stakeholders	PMP 3.4 Commit List	Plan Matrix, Entry Criteria	PMP 3.4 Commit List	PMP 3.4 Commit List	PMP 3.4 Commit List	PMP 3.4 Commit List	PMP 3.4 Commit List
GP2.8—Monitor and Control the Process	PMP 5	Plan Matrix, Exit Criteria	PMP 5	PMP 5	PMP 5	PMP 5	PMP 5
GP2.9—Objectively Evaluate Adherence	PMP 4.5.2	Plan Matrix, Exit Criteria	PMP 4.5.2	PMP 4.5.2	PMP 4.5.2	See Note*	PMP 4.5.2
GP2.10—Review Status with Higher Level Management	PMP 5	Plan Matrix, Exit Criteria	PMP 5	PMP 5	PMP 5	PMP 5	PMP 5

Note: PPQA GP 2.9—See Organization PPQA Plan Section.
Note: GP 2.2 for PP process area is a special case. GP 2.2 for PP has been satisfied by a planning matrix.

Next, let's consider assessing GP 3.2, which requires the organization to collect work products, measures and measurement results, and improvement information for all PAs. This does not mean 3 direct artifacts are required for all PAs for all projects, but that a representative sample should be provided. Rather than applying this practice to the extreme, appropriate judgment must be applied to determine reasonable evidence for practice implementation. By getting the big picture, a judgment can be made by the appraisal team as to whether additional evidence is needed or the practice is satisfied by the organization.

3.4.2.1 Doing the Math

After the artifacts and affirmations have been individually evaluated, it's time to come to some conclusions and begin the *Generate Appraisal Results* phase. This step need not wait for all data to be assembled. The team, or even mini-teams, should be continually looking at the scoring as the evaluation progresses.

This is one area that both combines and adds to the methods of the source model methods. The CBA-IPI called for more judgment, in part driven by the overlapping relationship between practices and goals. EIA 731-2 had a somewhat complex formula for calculating results based on the practice implementation at the organization level, but left it up to the teams to decide how to make the individual practice decisions that drove the calculations.

SCAMPI provides specific instructions on increasing levels of decision— implementation grading guidance for the project instantiations of each practice, rules on organizational results based on those decisions, and then additional rules for goal satisfaction and level ratings. At each level, there is room for judgment and defined boundaries. Starting with the practice instantiations, the team must decide whether the direct artifact is appropriate, whether indirect artifacts or affirmations provide support, and whether there are any significant weaknesses. At the organizational and goal level, the easy decisions are simple roll-ups of the individual practice instantiation scores. However, when implementation varies over the projects, or practices vary within a goal at the organizational level, there is a bounded range of judgment defined in the method. For instance, the decision for a practice characterized in a project instantiation as Not Implemented can still be judged Largely Implemented overall if there are also a significant number of Largely or

Fully Implemented scores. Particularly at the goal level, if there are weaknesses, a decision is required to determine whether or not when taken together they significantly affect the goal.

Once the goal satisfaction is determined, maturity or capability level rating is mostly determining which process areas have the specific goals and generic goals satisfied to what level. The model defines the requirements for each level. The two areas of minor complication are the maturity levels 4 and 5 and the application of advanced practices in capability levels.[9]

For maturity levels 4 and 5, a determination must be made as to which sub-processes the practices in the level 4 and 5 process areas are applied. For instance, is quantitative management applied to sub-processes in requirements management, verification, or some other process area?

Treatment of advanced practices is carefully explained in the method. However, they are seldom a factor. They only appear in the technical process areas and are limited in number. There are few cases where appraisals are concerned with specific practice performance at lower levels.

The overall objective of the SCAMPI scoring method is to give the ability to interpret what the team sees while giving some guidance and limits on how to turn a large number of observations into a final story. The rules narrow the bounds of what can be decided, but the team still has quite a bit of discretion to reach a final decision.

3.4.2.2 Validating Gaps

After the team reaches initial conclusions about findings, the participants must be given an opportunity to respond. It wouldn't be a good idea to proceed directly to a final briefing and have someone say, "That's not true!"

Although SCAMPI does not specifically address it, individual reviews with the project leads using a listing of the findings is an effective way to get dialogue on them. This is a method of implementing the "survey instrument" approach in SCAMPI. These sessions can be effectively done by mini-teams.

---

[9] For an explanation of advanced practices see, for example, *CMMI Distilled*, Section 7.3 on the engineering process areas.

Another way to use the preliminary findings to remove uncertainties is to include statements that would benefit from additional input for certainty. This must be done with the consensus of the whole team.

3.4.2.3 Re-plan Data Collection

This is the one path that can return to the planning activities. It can occur at any time during the collection and review of evidence. If additional artifacts are identified as needed or interviews are changed, the team needs to update the record of the plan. It is possible to actually reduce the inputs needed. This may happen when a very conservative approach was included in the initial plan. In particular, some interviews have been either eliminated or reduced in length. If the plan requires changes to the length or scope of the appraisal, sponsor approval is required.

3.4.2.4 A Few Notes on Notes

One of the most difficult compromises in conducting a SCAMPI is how much effort to put into note taking. Certainly, the method is quite specific on the minimums, which are rather comprehensive. The requirement for *all* team members to take specific notes on *all* references within model scope generates a significant amount of data. Adding extensive notes on artifacts can overwhelm a team. However, this is not nearly as exasperating as entering a discussion on a finding and not being able to trace a significant proposed finding to the source!

The flexibility is primarily found in the treatment of artifacts. Because the team can go back in discussions and review what is there, the importance of quoting verbatim is reduced. Also, the evidence seen by a mini-team can be brought before the whole team if needed. A clear reference that points to a specific part of an artifact and notes the significance is sufficient. If the evidence is not considered appropriate, the rationale is essential for later discussions.

3.5 And in Conclusion

The final *Report Results* phase includes both delivering the final results (presentations, reports, and so on) and also packaging and archiving the appraisal assets.

3.5.1 Stand and Deliver

It's time for the big finale! The final presentation can be a very stressful time. If the process improvement efforts were successful and the results meet or exceed expectations, it can be quite a party. If the results fall short, it's a bit of a wet blanket. In any case, there are some specific actions that will occur at this time. The most obvious is the presentation of appraisal results to the sponsor and the organization. The new wrinkle is the Appraisal Disclosure Statement.

3.5.1.1 The Big Show

The final presentation generally is a summary of the appraisal findings, and it also includes a summary of the appraisal process. To some it may come as a surprise that inclusion of the ratings is optional. This is more likely to be the case in an external evaluation than an internal assessment. Since the scope of the appraisal is usually well known and supporting findings for any model component deemed Unsatisfied must be reported, the ratings can generally be derived from the required information. So while ratings may be optional in the final presentation, generally there is seldom a reason to follow that option, especially for an internal appraisal. Ratings will be provided for the components that the appraisal plan identifies as items to be rated.

The stress in a final presentation can be seen in the reaction of one organization when the presentation included a chart on "where we were last time" before the current continuous ratings profile. Although the lead appraiser noted what was coming and the chart was clearly titled, the team feared a call to 911 might be needed from the gasp in the room when the audience saw a low score when it was expecting to see the current results. There was immense relief when the chart quickly passed and success showed up on the screen.

3.5.1.2 Truth in Advertising

Suspicions abound about organizations getting a rating for a small group and subsequently claiming that rating for the entire organization. While it won't completely prevent that from happening, the Appraisal Disclosure Statement (ADS) does provide an element of truth-in-advertising to the appraisal results. The key contents of the statement are as follows:

- Who did the appraisal
- When it happened
- What organizational unit and which domains were included
- What version of CMMI was used, including which process areas were rated
- What maturity or capability levels were assigned

As part of the final presentation, the lead appraiser presents the sponsor with the ADS summary of what happened. If a small group obtains a capability level 3 rating on a single Process Area, the ADS will so state. This doesn't stop the organization from claiming "We're Level 3!" in their next proposal. However, it docs allow a savvy customer to ask for the proof and see whether the claim is actually relevant to the part of the organization from which the proposal comes.

SCAMPI provides for tailoring due to legal concerns when used in the evaluation mode as part of a source selection. It is recognized that the timing and nature of any information to bidders has additional constraints beyond the method.

3.5.1.3 The Executive Session

The SCAMPI method shows an executive session as following the formal presentation and being optional. Doing it, and furthermore doing it first, is the best approach in most situations. When done early, the sponsor has an opportunity to become prepared for the open disclosure of the results, good or bad. Since the success of process improvement is very much dependent on the support of the sponsor, their comments at the end of an appraisal can be critical to the continuation of progress. The original concern was that the sponsor might try to amend the results prior to the final presentation. While occasionally this may occur, the lead has the responsibility and authority to hold fast. The benefit of a prepared sponsor at the final presentation also outweighs this risk by a large margin.

3.5.1.4 What's Next?

Planning for next steps is another optional activity in SCAMPI. Even if the desired rating is achieved, hopefully the organization will continue to progress using as guidance the weaknesses and "opportunities to improve" that were identified. A good way to get started is to take advantage of the insight and expertise of the assembled appraisal team.

Often they have additional data and suggestions that would be very advantageous in taking action. However, some of the learning will fade quickly with time and external team members may not be available for future efforts.

3.5.1.5 How Long Are Results Valid?

This question is asked frequently, especially with regard to ratings. In some cases, customers have asked for appraisals to be no older than two years.

One answer is (as we said earlier) not even as long as it takes the ink to dry on the ADS. The intent of the CMMI approach is to establish a culture that will automatically continue to apply the processes. This state can and often will persist. However, there are many cases where management has (to one degree or another) abandoned the process focus as soon as the score is obtained. You may see an immediate dismissal of the process group under the assumption that the goal has been reached and no further effort is required. However, the process infrastructure needs maintenance as much as any other system. The result is twofold. First, the actual performance backslides and usage of the processes degrades or stops completely. Second, the benefits degrade or stop as well. It doesn't make a lot of sense to spend the amount it takes to achieve a level, and then abandon the task just when the return on investment is about to start. However, if process improvement is sold as getting to a level rather than operating at it, management may take away that impression. To avoid this, the process improvement group needs to be clear on the long-term business case and the maintenance and support costs and benefits.

Another answer is that in many organizations it would be unthinkable, after the extensive effort and investment that went into the appraisal, to make abrupt changes to something that has proven benefits for the long-term health of the organization. Many organizations have experienced pain due to failings in the process arena; perhaps complaints from an irate customer, or a missed schedule, or a cost overrun, or an unhappy end user. These may be among the reasons that the organization had for investing in process improvement and CMMI. The ink on the ADS would be very expensive indeed if there was no value to be obtained other than the brief use of a number. So in many cases, thinking of a CMMI rating as good for a year or two is not unreasonable.

3.5.2 Package and Archive

It isn't over until the paperwork is done—or electronic equivalent! Before the lead appraiser can go home, the final appraisal record must be put together, data must be provided to the CMMI Steward, and artifacts should be archived (if needed).

3.5.2.1 Lessons Learned

Having the appraisal team create a collection of lessons learned is an optional practice. However, it is highly recommended for any lead appraiser or organization that anticipates ever doing it again. Lessons can be minor (as what worked for lunch) or significant (as concerns about how tools or web access to data significantly helped or hindered the quality or efficiency of the appraisal). While the activity of documenting lessons learned is listed at the end of the method description, it has also been very effective to have incremental feedback sessions on a regular basis throughout the appraisal while things still are fresh in the participants' minds. This approach also permits corrective action in real time.

3.5.2.2 Getting the Record Straight

The details of what was reviewed and decided are recorded for future reference. Please note that the required record contents includes "objective evidence, or identification thereof, sufficient to substantiate goal rating judgments."[10] A complete library of all evidence submitted for the appraisal need not be retained in perpetuity for the appraisal record. The record only has to identify what the team observed that justified the goal ratings. If a dozen artifacts were submitted for each practice for each program and the team took the time to look at a majority of them but only a key few of them were necessary to establish a decision, then list those in the record.

Actually, this task is made a lot simpler by automated tools that record data reviewed, findings, etc. When all of this is recorded in the tool, the actual record generation is limited to some additional data such as the plan and ADS.

---

[10] MDD, 3.2.

3.5.2.3 Feedback to the CMMI Steward

This is one of the places that the method is not completely explicit and the CMMI Steward is expected to provide the details. It is recognized that the Steward must have the authority to request information as necessary to maintain the quality of the appraisal program, including Lead Appraiser authorization.

3.5.2.4 Archive and Dispose

After all is said and done, the organization must archive or dispose of the various materials generated during the appraisal. In some cases, it is helpful to retain notes to support follow-up actions. However, access to such notes must be limited to the original appraisal team members so that confidentiality is maintained.

The question often asked by management is "How will I know where to apply corrective action if you don't tell me who is messing up?" Remember that in a level 3 or higher assessment, the findings will be across the organization and fixes will generally apply to more than one place. Also, the appraisal team members usually include some of the local process team, at least in assessment mode, and they will be able to help guide the direction of the fixes. And if the organization isn't approaching level 3, a full-up SCAMPI A may not be a good fit anyway.

3.6 Summary

The insight provided here should help with conduct of a more effective and efficient SCAMPI A appraisal. As noted, attention to planning and monitoring the appraisal will pay off through more complete and accurate information with less effort. However, there is a sizable minimum of data and decisions required for a full SCAMPI A. The next chapter presents the shorter Class B and Class C appraisal methods that should be used for less involved checks of process maturity either leading to a SCAMPI A or when a rating is not a required outcome.

Chapter 4

SCAMPI Class B and C Appraisal Methods

fat-free scam·pi an appraisal in which the objective
evidence presented to the team is very thin
mel·on scam·pi an appraisal conducted by SEI folks from Pittsburgh

The prominence of appraisal ratings in today's competitive environment has grown steadily since the 1980s as more acquirers and customers search for reliable discriminators to aid in their decision making. For the providers who must do everything to establish such credentials to carry them through the competition, the pursuit of these widely coveted outcomes has become a very high-stakes game. In order to respond to this situation, many consultants and internal appraisers created their own version of the "official" methods in an effort to provide more frequent and less costly insight about the process maturity status of organizations. While the benchmarking-oriented appraisals tend to receive the most visibility, the less intrusive and less costly alternatives to the benchmarking appraisal are actually used much more frequently. This trend in the community is what led the CMMI Product Development Team to call for three different classes of appraisal methods in the Appraisal Requirements for CMMI (ARC v1.1).

The majority of this book focuses on the so-called class A method, referred to as SCAMPI A here. However, two new methods that strive to codify the best practices from non-benchmarking appraisals developed over the years are also available as members of the family of SCAMPI appraisal methods. The class B and class C versions of SCAMPI are intended to support organizations in deriving reliable insights toward their efforts to improve performance on the process capability/maturity dimension. While these methods serve a variety of needs, the intent is to offer an integrated suite of methods that build on one another as organizations use them over time. Therefore, the SCAMPI C method, the least rigorous of the three, includes tailoring options that support more efficient and effective SCAMPI B appraisals conducted after the results of the SCAMPI C have been used. Similarly, SCAMPI B appraisals can be performed in a way that reduces the burden of the data collection of the SCAMPI A appraisal. In each of these cases, it is also expected that the outcome of the previous appraisal will build confidence in anticipating the outcome of the subsequent appraisal—that is, these are upwardly compatible appraisal results.

The key differentiation among these three methods, when used as a family (SCAMPI C, B, and A), lies in the focus of their investigation. In this configuration, the SCAMPI C method might focus on examining the approach to implementing practices that support (when they are implemented) achievement of the desired end-state reflected in the goals of CMMI. In contrast, the SCAMPI B method might focus on examining deployed practices for weaknesses that would prevent achievement of the desired end-state reflected in the goals, if the deployed practices were institutionalized across the organizational unit. Finally, the SCAMPI A method focuses on examining the institutionalization of practices across a coherent sample of the organizational unit to judge whether or not the desired end-state reflected in the goals has actually been achieved. These three different foci can be examined in progression as an organization designs, deploys, and then institutionalizes a set of practices. Alternatively, these different foci may reflect different needs for stakeholders in the outcome of an appraisal process; stakeholders with different perspectives and/or different relationships to the organizational unit being appraised. Finally, the distinctions among Approach, Deployment, and Institutionalization are intended to define the nature of conclusions to be drawn from performing the appraisal, and not a limit on the type of data that may be used as an input to the appraisal. For example, there is no reason why artifacts from implemented practices cannot be used in a SCAMPI C.

4.1 SCAMPI C Method Overview

When a minimally intrusive approach is needed, the SCAMPI C method permits detailed examination of the process used or intended for use (even future use) in an organization. Because there is no requirement to view artifacts resulting directly from implementation of the process, a very wide range of applications can be devised. The relaxed requirements for data collection permit anything from a pure questionnaire-based approach to an interview and documentation intensive approach—all conducted by a single appraiser. A very minimalist implementation of this method is quite rare, as most experienced appraisers will rarely limit data collection to a single source.

This method allows more extensive tailoring than the other two SCAMPI methods. However, this method supports a narrower range of applications than SCAMPI B. An acquisition organization that is "down selecting" from a large number of suppliers can use SCAMPI C, with a focus on review of process standards, to determine which subset of suppliers warrants a more detailed process appraisal. An organization preparing to tackle a new set of process areas in the CMMI can verify the fidelity of its approach before starting the deployment. As an interim appraisal, SCAMPI C can be used to periodically examine the fidelity of the implemented practices to the intended approach—this would incorporate examination of direct artifacts of implementation, which is a tailoring option. Frequently, the most significant reason a SCAMPI C is selected is the desire to use a single appraiser for efficiency.

4.2 SCAMPI B Method Overview

When conclusions about actual implementation of practices are needed but benchmark quality outputs would be overkill, the SCAMPI B method provides a more rigorous method than the SCAMPI C method, and with more flexibility than SCAMPI A permits. This method requires the use of a team and the examination of artifacts that result directly from the implementation of practices. While standards for sampling and establishing completeness of data are relaxed, the results of the SCAMPI B resemble the strengths and weaknesses seen as a standard output of the SCAMPI A method. Many uses of this method differ only slightly from the "full-blown" SCAMPI A method.

This method may have the highest utility in that it can be tailored to cover the widest range of usage scenarios. An acquisition organization monitoring the process improvement programs within its supplier chain uses this method to get focused information on the practices used on the projects they fund. As a dress-rehearsal for a benchmarking appraisal, members of an engineering process group use this method to provide a readiness check for their management stakeholders. To serve as a means of monitoring and refocusing the deployment of new practices in a large organization, this method can be tailored to include more rigorous sampling standards like the SCAMPI A—without requiring the same level of data sufficiency in areas viewed as a lower priority. Often, a SCAMPI B is selected primarily to remove the pressure and stigma associated with a benchmarking output.

4.3 Using the Integrated Suite of SCAMPI Methods

The SCAMPI methods differ from other ARC-conformant methods in that they are designed around a common data structure, which is tied closely to the structure of the CMMI. Upward compatibility of appraisal artifacts is achieved through tailoring options that address reuse of outputs on subsequent appraisals, predictive statements about future appraisal results, and increasing precision and accuracy with each subsequent appraisal. Concerns relating to continuity of the organization and the appraisal team, as well as the expectation of a "learning effect" in the organization over time, affect operational choices to be made in planning the appraisals. The fundamental aspect of the appraisal methods that permits their use as an integrated suite is the common data structure and data dictionary.

Tailoring options for the SCAMPI methods support upward compatibility in order to permit reuse of appraisal artifacts, anticipation of subsequent appraisal results, and improvement in precision and accuracy with repeated appraisals. The option to re-evaluate and revise the set of Practice Implementation Indicators over a series of interactive sessions is one of the most obvious ways upward compatibility can be realized. As the understanding of the existing and desired process (if they differ) grows clearer, the appraisal results grow more precise in identifying and predicting the barriers to success. This allows the improvement program to be informed with feedback that improves in reliability, specificity, and accuracy over time.

Operationally, this requires a plan for a sequence of appraisals that addresses issues relating to continuity of organizational unit and appraisal participants, the progress of improvement between appraisals, and the evolution of appraisal outputs and their precision. When the definition of the organizational unit evolves over time, as more roles and responsibilities are accounted for in the defined processes, the reliability of appraisal results may be affected by this threat to continuity. As well, the progress made in improving the process may occur at different rates, depending on the issue under consideration. As the organization's level of sophistication in process analysis grows over time, the level of precision and reliability in appraisal outputs will also grow. Harmonizing the appraisal and improvement activities is the key to using the SCAMPI methods in this way.

The data structure common to the SCAMPI family of appraisals is embodied in the paradigm of *Practice Implementation Indicators* (PII). This structure can be used in organizing the input to the appraisal process, the data used within the appraisal process and/or the data provided as an output from the appraisal process. None of the SCAMPI methods require that the input be structured in this way, though this tailoring option for SCAMPI A is viewed as a promising source of efficiency. Every SCAMPI method uses this paradigm to identify objective evidence as Direct Artifacts, Indirect Artifacts, or Affirmations. As well, each item of evidence is identified with the model practice and project or instance from which it derives. There is no requirement that the PIIs used by the team be preserved as an output of the appraisal process, though this option is obviously key to the use of this artifact over time. Organizations have devised other uses for a database that documents how the implemented process within an organizational unit or project corresponds to the practices in a reference model like CMMI.

The flexibility to tailor the degree to which the PII structure is used for inputs and outputs of the appraisal is a key enabler to the compatibility of the SCAMPI methods with one another. Some organizations are able to create mappings of this type to their organization standard process at a very detailed level, then maintain traceability at the project instance level as well. Using such an infrastructure, it is possible to integrate process management and process appraisal activities to avoid labor-intensive documentation mapping performed in many organizations, for the sole purpose of satisfying appraisal teams.

4.4 Using SCAMPI Methods as "Stand Alone"

The SCAMPI B and SCAMPI C methods have a wide range of utility beyond their use in a succession, as described previously. There are numerous situations that provide opportunities for "stand alone" usage of each of these methods. Many different descriptors exist for non-benchmarking appraisals, including "mini-appraisal," "gap-analysis," "getting started workshop," and "improvement monitoring appraisals." The ways in which the SCAMPI B and C methods are tailored to perform these types of appraisals is described in the following paragraphs.

4.4.1 The Mini-Appraisal

Using a SCAMPI B, mini-appraisals are typically performed as an alternative to a benchmarking appraisal when the generation of ratings is not required. In most uses, the appraisal event will resemble the benchmarking appraisal in many respects. In fact, a mini-appraisal is often used as a "dress rehearsal" for a benchmarking appraisal. A mini-appraisal can also be used between the conduct of benchmarking appraisals in order to provide status and to focus improvement on additional areas of weakness.

Using a SCAMPI C, the mini-appraisal is most often an "expert-mode" appraisal. Because a class C method does not require use of a team, many professional consultants use this method to provide a low-cost alternative to a team-based activity. In this usage, the mini-appraisal may last a single day, or as much as two weeks. Many of the traditional elements of the benchmarking appraisal are omitted in order to minimize resource requirements, but also because the single expert appraiser is typically very skilled. This type of appraisal is often referred to as a "quick look" and the preferences of the single appraiser will shape the event almost entirely.

Regardless of the class of the appraisal (SCAMPI B versus SCAMPI C) the defining characteristics of the mini-appraisal include a focus on getting a relatively complete set of results while minimizing time and resource requirements. Mini-appraisals are frequently used to anticipate a future benchmarking appraisal or take the place of a benchmarking appraisal when ratings are not needed. Any process improvement program involving substantial investments of time and resources likely includes use of the mini-appraisal to gather information by using lower-cost methods than the traditional benchmarking appraisal. Results of mini-appraisals are frequently combined to build a composite of strengths and weaknesses incrementally, over time, across process areas of the model, or across sub-units within the organization.

4.4.2 The Gap Analysis

The name gap analysis is used to cover a broad set of appraisal activities. In fact, what some people call a mini-appraisal is considered a gap analysis to others. The difference between how SCAMPI C is used in the performance of a gap analysis and its use as a mini-appraisal is not significant. A gap analysis performed using SCAMPI B, on the other hand, is likely to involve a more narrowly defined scope of the model than the mini-appraisal typically would.

A gap analysis is applied to address a well-defined scope of the model. This approach can focus on a subset of the model that had previously been found to be inadequately addressed using a benchmarking appraisal. This use of the method is often referred to as a "delta appraisal" as the focus is on changes that have been made following a benchmarking appraisal that identified significant weaknesses. Process improvement sponsors can use this method to ensure that weaknesses preventing achievement of a target rating have been addressed, so the next benchmarking appraisal will likely find that the target rating has been achieved.

4.4.3 Getting Started Workshop

This type of appraisal is more like a consulting event than the other appraisal types discussed here. Typically, the primary goal is to provide information and advice to help initiate an improvement program in an organization. It is not very common that a SCAMPI B is used for this purpose, as qualified team members are not very likely to be available in such an organization. The SCAMPI C method provides maximum flexibility in structuring this event, and can be conducted by a single person.

Often an extended training session or a series of interactions following a formal training course is used to conduct this type of appraisal. Interviews of a cross section of staff or the use of a change readiness survey are examples of techniques available for this type of appraisal. Very limited formal outputs are typically expected, and the experience of discussing issues and identifying priorities is what the organization often expects.

4.4.4 Improvement Monitoring

This appraisal type relies on the existence of an existing improvement program and is typically focused on the priorities established in that program. Whether it be used in a supplier-acquirer relationship or in the context of an internal corporate initiative, the defining characteristic of this type of appraisal is that it relates to specific targets for improvement for the appraised organization. Use of this method in an acquisition setting might limit the focus to a single project. Use in a corporate program might rely on a predefined set of milestones for the improvement effort. The results of the appraisal provide a status report on the ongoing improvement effort, and require an external context (external to the appraisal event) to interpret the appraisal outcomes. Award fees or other incentives may be associated with the outcome of this type of appraisal, though a benchmarking appraisal (SCAMPI A) is better suited for this type of high-value discriminator.

Example Using Multiple Appraisals

Few organizations, if any, would elect to do all the appraisals listed here. Most organizations willing to use appraisals in this way would do one or two of these events before going into a benchmarking appraisal. Large organizations might use a greater variety and number of appraisals like these. The list of appraisals and attributes below provides a starting point for readers who wish to understand how a set of customized events can be used in sequence.

Getting Started Intervention—SCAMPI C—Five Days

- Introductory training

- Mapping exercise

- Involve stakeholders and practitioners

- Tie into ISO or other legacy quality management systems (if possible)

- Deliver action plan

Mini-Appraisal—SCAMPI C+ or B—Three Days

- Look at first deployments
- Understand differences from approach
- Plan correction and further deployment

Gap Analysis—SCAMPI B—4 Days

- Readiness for upcoming benchmark
- Rigorous data collection and analysis
- Risk identification for next phase

Mini-Appraisal—SCAMPI B+—Five Days

- Dress-rehearsal for benchmark
- Do everything like the A, but "less"
- Go/No-go decision at the end

Benchmark—SCAMPI A—Eight Days

Chapter 5

SCAMPI for Internal Process Improvement

squash scam·pi an appraisal conducted by upper management
***all-you-can-eat scam·pi** an appraisal in which the team is swamped*
with objective evidence for every model subpractice

This chapter discusses some aspects of using SCAMPI for internal process improvement, especially those aspects that are new to the process community as a result of CMMI or SCAMPI. Note that in this and the following chapter the term "appraisal" is used for both internal process improvement and external audits. These two uses of the appraisal methods were previously termed "assessment" and "evaluation," upholding the tradition of the maturity modeling community to consider every word in the English language to be reserved.

SCAMPI is a means of examining an organization's processes. By using CMMI as a reference model, it is possible to objectively and methodically analyze an organization's processes and identify its strengths and weaknesses. This analysis helps the organization target its process improvement activities to maximize effectiveness. Periodic appraisals then enable an organization to track its process improvement progress and refine its process improvement plans. For an organization that is serious about continuous process improvement, appraisals are a way of life. CMMI appraisals focus on identifying improvement opportunities; however, in addition to using appraisal findings to improve processes, organizations use appraisals to benchmark their progress in process improvement for both internal purposes and with their customers and suppliers.

The SCAMPI appraisal method was developed to meet the requirement that appraisals under CMMI be more efficient than *combined* appraisals using the source models. Thus, a CMMI software and systems engineering appraisal must be shorter and less costly than a software engineering appraisal using the SW-CMM *plus* a systems engineering appraisal that uses EIA 731. This does not mean that a SCAMPI A appraisal will be shorter and less costly than a single SW-CMM appraisal. In fact, as noted earlier, SCAMPI A appraisals are typically more costly and time consuming simply due to the additional breadth of the material and organizations appraised.

In addition, the SCAMPI A method is intended to produce less variation in appraisal performance; for example, it is more rigorous, hence potentially more costly. Recent comparisons, however, do shed some light on SCAMPI A performance. When comparing the cost and performance of SCAMPI A and CBA-IPI using the same capability maturity model (SW-CMM), Ron Radice[1] found that

- SCAMPI A is more focused on data management, verification, and validation
- Appraisal team management is basically the same
- SCAMPI A has reduced variation in method performance
- SCAMPI A is more costly, but the differences are small, as seen in Ron's[1] table

In Calendar Days

SW-CMM Level 5 Appraisal

Organization Size	CBA-IPI Document Review	CBA-IPI Onsite	SCAMPI A Document Review	SCAMPI A Onsite
<50	1-2	<5	2	<5
50-100	1-2	5	2	5
100-250	2	5	2-3	5
>250	2-3	>5	3-4	>5

---

[1] Radice, Ron. "SCAMPI with SW-CMM," delivered at Software Technology Conference, Salt Lake City, April 30, 2003.

5.1 Preparation Is Critical

The objectives of performing a SCAMPI appraisal for internal process improvement are to set the stage, determine the state of process implementation, and help establish priorities for process improvement in an organization. Diagnoses from SCAMPI appraisals should be part of a deliberate improvement cycle, such as Deming's Plan-Do-Check-Act or the SEI's IDEAL^{SM} cycle. In the IDEAL cycle, which is described in detail in Chapter 7, "SCAMPI Implementation Issues," appraisals are used in the Diagnosing phase. The IDEAL cycle follows a planned Initiation phase that sets the context, including business case, and establishes sponsorship and a process improvement infrastructure.

When CMMI models are used for enterprise process improvement, as is their focus, several considerations affect the success (and cost) of the effort that may be different from those in a single discipline improvement effort, such as software engineering. The size of the models and the inclusion of new disciplines make the planning process even more important and more difficult.

Key questions include the following: Should we have an appraisal? Should we do it now or later? Should Systems Engineering and Software Engineering be appraised together with separate results, or should their appraisals be integrated? Which appraisal class should be used? A set of appraisal classes is defined based on appraisal usage scenarios. For an organization just starting on the path to enterprise process improvement, the recommended path is to start with a Class C appraisal to appraise the approach. This should be followed by a Class B appraisal analyzing initial deployment. If a rating is desired or a more rigorous and in-depth investigation of your processes is needed, use a SCAMPI A appraisal. This C-B-A cycle can then be continued to manage process improvement through each phase of the IDEAL cycle.

What should be included in each appraisal? It depends on the business objectives of the organization and should be planned as part of your CMMI implementation strategy.

Expanding on some of these questions, the organization and Lead Appraiser should consider

- **Organization scope:** The improvement effort might now include groups and individuals that have not been part of process improvement efforts before. It might also include groups that have used different models and appraisal methods, such as EIA 731 or ISO. Effort must be taken to involve and educate all relevant stakeholders regarding the reasons and goals of all of the activities.

- **Model Scope:** Model scope includes the process areas and generic goals that will be examined during the appraisal. Again, your organization's business objectives, as well as the current state of process focus in the organization, will be valuable in deciding on model scope.

- **Size:** The inclusion of various disciplines could cause an increase in appraisal audience size that is unprecedented in the organization and for which the appraisal team is unprepared. Interviews and objective evidence verification will present challenges to the team.

- **Disciplines:** As disciplines are added to the appraisal, appraisal team members with specific knowledge of those disciplines will be needed. This has been observed already using SCAMPI for combined SE/SW appraisals. As more disciplines are included within the scope, it may become very challenging to staff the team. In addition, organizational issues can exacerbate problems with the appraisal of different disciplines, and may even necessitate multiple appraisals.

- **Improvement Status:** The appraisal sponsor and planners will need knowledge of current process improvement efforts and their statuses. For instance, appraising a neophyte group combined with a high-maturity group could have the potential of a drop in the performance of the whole organization and could force decisions to be made on how to perform the appraisal and report the results. In this instance, the groups might start using separate appraisals and then integrating as the lower-level group improves.

Prior to performing a SCAMPI A appraisal, the following Readiness Check should be performed.

Readiness Check	Criteria
Action Plans	Have all actions in current process improvement plans been completed satisfactorily? If not, how might this affect the appraisal? Are all appropriate PAs covered? What Capability Level or Maturity Level is being appraised, if any?

Readiness Check	Criteria
Documentation Review	Do the organization and projects have a sufficient base of documentation? Do process documentation and implementation evidence exist? Has a review of the documentation indicated an acceptable level of risk?
Institutionalization	Are the processes part of the organization's culture? Is there a sufficient infrastructure in place (policies, training, resources, measurements, and oversight)? Have the processes been executed enough times that they have become the standard way of doing business?
Informal Appraisal	Have recent informal appraisals (Class C and B) confirmed that there are no serious weaknesses?

5.2 The Appraisal Team

After an organization decides to schedule SCAMPI internal appraisals, the appraisal team should start being formed and trained. Successful appraisal teams require

- A plan, including objectives, constraints, scope, outputs, tailoring, resources, cost, schedule, logistics, risks, and commitment
- Clearly defined goals
- Clearly defined roles
- Established rules of engagement
- Well-defined decision procedures
- Understanding of the group process
- Clear communications
- Proper team behavior
- Balanced participation
- Training

5.2.1 Training

Training requirements for the team include model and appraisal training and must be planned far enough in advance to schedule attendance at an "Intro to CMMI" course for all team members. Appraisal team training can then be taught by the team lead. For SCAMPI A appraisals, each team must be led by an SEI authorized Lead Appraiser. For Class B and C appraisals, the ARC only requires the leader to have training and experience—it doesn't specify what type of training. We recommend either a SCAMPI Lead Appraiser or a person with extensive experience in CMMI and either SCAMPI or CBA IPI appraisal team experience lead these teams.

5.2.2 Team Composition

Team composition for SCAMPI appraisals using CMMI models may be different from CBA IPI teams. Because CMMI is used for enterprise improvement, a much broader range of knowledge might be required on the team. A SCAMPI A team typically has four to nine members, but every discipline being assessed must be represented on the team with appropriate experience in that discipline. The SCAMPI A Method Definition Document requires a team average of six years of engineering experience with a team total of at least 25 years of experience. In addition, the team must have a total of 10 years of management experience with at least one member having a minimum of six years of experience as a manager. Team members should also have good oral and written communication skills and, most importantly, have the ability to perform as team players and negotiate consensus.

In addition to the team members, a member of the appraised organization should help plan and facilitate the appraisal. However, a person who manages people or processes in the organization or who may be directly affected by the appraisal outcome *should not* be a team member.

5.2.3 Team Personalities

Another aspect of team composition is personality, especially for the mini-teams—those small (two to three person) teams that analyze data and generate findings for a slice of the model or the organization. We have found through (sometimes painful) experience that knowledge of our teammates' personality types can facilitate rapid movement through the formative phases of team evolution and prevent disaster as the team struggles with the appraisal.

The *Myers-Briggs Type Indicator* (MBTI[2]) is a valuable tool that groups people according to their personality styles in four dimensions: Extroverted versus Introverted (E versus I), Sensors versus Intuitives (S versus N), Thinking versus Feeling (T versus F), and Judging versus Perceiving (J versus P). In our experience, the last characteristic, Judging versus Perceiving, has the most impact on the performance of appraisal teams. Suppose four people are organized in two mini-teams, composed of JJ and PP people. The PP team carefully considers all data and continually asks for more, resisting the temptation to actually produce results—delaying the whole team consensus process as they ask for more and more. The JJ team, however, makes up its mind after reviewing one document and interviewing one person. They sit and shout at the other mini-team to get with the program. A better approach would be to form the teams with one J and one P each. Provided they don't kill each other during the appraisal, each member will balance the other to produce reliable results within the time constraints of the appraisal. In general

- Introverts need to try to participate more
- Extroverts need to try not to dominate
- Don't rush to closure and be unwilling to consider new information
- *However,* closure *must* be reached within the team's timeline
- The appraisal process is data driven
- *However,* don't get lost in the details

5.2.4 Consensus

Decision making on appraisal teams is done by consensus, not unanimous vote nor majority vote. Consensus is finding a proposal acceptable enough that all team members can support it or live with it, with no team member opposing it. It attempts to produce a win-win solution for all team members and allows the team to retain team integrity and mission focus. At times, the consensus process can require several cycles through the decision cycle shown in Figure 5-1 as the team continues to gather and analyze factual information bearing on a decision.

---

[2] MBTI, Myers-Briggs, and Myers-Briggs Type Indicator are registered trademarks or trademarks of the Myers-Briggs Type Indicator Trust in the United States and other countries.

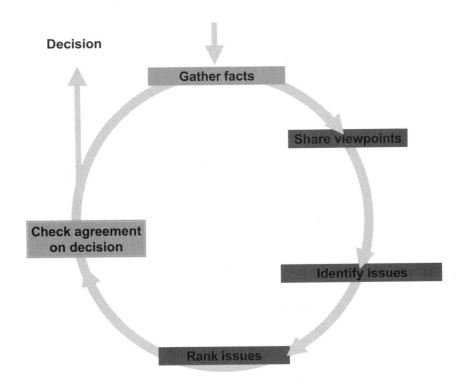

Figure 5-1: *The Consensus Process*

If consensus cannot be obtained, a decision should not be forced, such as through a majority vote. The item under consideration must be left not rated.

5.3 The Appraisal Team's Timeline

Starting with the decision to perform any SCAMPI appraisal, the appraisal team follows a timeline like the one shown in Figure 5-2, including getting organized, developing the appraisal plan, obtaining required training, performing the appraisal, and following up.

An example SCAMPI A schedule, including a "week-in-the-life" of the appraisal, is shown in Figure 5-3 and follows the overall timeline.

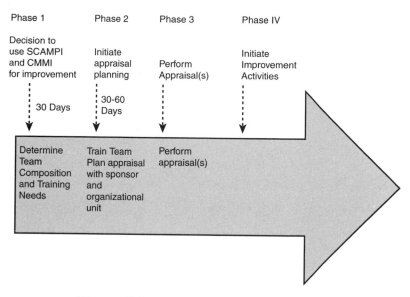

Figure 5-2: *SCAMPI Appraisal Schedule*

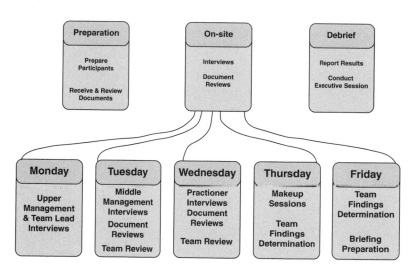

Figure 5-3: *The Appraisal Team's Timeline*

Chapter 6

SCAMPI for External Audits

> ***pork scam·pi*** *an appraisal conducted by the government*
> ***squid scam·pi*** *an appraisal in which the objective evidence is hard to find*

As provided in ISO 15504, SCAMPI appraisals may be used for external audits (termed external appraisals in this chapter) as well as internal appraisals. External appraisals are used by companies in selecting and monitoring their suppliers as well as by government acquisition organizations in supplier selection and contract process monitoring. They are especially used during the acquisition of a major software-intensive system where lives, fortunes, or national defense are at stake, such as a new tank, an upgraded aircraft flight control system, or an employee pay and management system. Because appraisals are widely used by government organizations, and the U.S. government has the most stringent rules for acquisition (the *Federal Acquisition Regulations*, or FAR), this chapter describes appraisals in this framework. Industry use of external appraisals might follow similar but different schedules and methods of use.

While some would say that examining the supplier's processes smacks of telling them how to develop the system, acquirers and users often feel that they have a right to expect a professional approach to the development of systems critical to them. Mature processes are one indication of the professionalism of the supplier's team. Appraisals also help acquisition managers do the following:

- Identify risks during supplier selection
- Manage risk by motivating suppliers to follow and improve development processes
- Monitor award fee incentives for suppliers who have structured process improvement programs

In addition, acquisition organizations become knowledgeable of the benefits of process improvement and the role they have in successful acquisition efforts while working with their development organizations. As some acquirers have found, this knowledge encouraged them to engage in acquisition process improvement in parallel with their suppliers' improvement efforts.

6.1 Appraisal Objectives

The use of SCAMPI by acquirers typically has different objectives from internal process improvement. Developers pursue process improvement to improve their productivity and bottom line as well as their time, effort, and performance estimation capability. Acquirers are primarily interested in cost, schedule, and performance risk reduction.

To reduce the risk in the acquisition of large software-intensive systems, U.S. government organizations have been using multiple tools to evaluate supplier processes in the recent past. These include *Software Capability Evaluations* (SCE^{SM}), based on the Software CMM, *Software Development Capacity Evaluations* (SDCEs), and the FAA-iCMM, used by the Federal Aviation Agency.

SCEs are being superceded by SCAMPI appraisals as CMMI models are replacing the SW-CMM for process improvement and process characterization. SDCE evaluations are based on a customizable questionnaire filled out by each bidder, followed by optional site visits. SDCEs are also being superceded by SCAMPI appraisals as both the developer and acquisition communities move to a single tool.

6.2 Requirements for External Appraisals

External appraisals are performed for source selection and for contract performance monitoring. Under the FAR, the sponsor for an appraisal for source selection is normally the *Source Selection Authority* (SSA).

However, the lead appraiser and the appraisal team typically do not spend a lot of time with the actual sponsor planning the appraisal. In most government source selections, the SCAMPI team is one of a number of teams involved in providing information to an Evaluation Board. This board reports evaluations of proposals, as compared with a *Request for Proposals* (RFP), along with process appraisal results, to an Advisory Council, reporting to the Source Selection Authority, who makes the final selection.

In preparing for the appraisal, the SCAMPI team follows a timeline such as the one in Figure 6-1.

It is essential that the decision to use SCAMPI appraisals during a government source selection allow at least four to five weeks to determine the appraisal requirements. These requirements must be included in acquisition strategy documents and the RFP. In addition, the *Federal Business Opportunity* (FBO)/*Commerce Business Daily* (CBD) announcement of the procurement must include notification of the intent to perform a SCAMPI appraisal.

During this planning phase, the scope and form of the appraisal must be determined. Scope includes the model representation (staged or continuous), the disciplines to be appraised, the Process Areas included, as well as maturity level or capability level determinations, and the organizational units to be appraised. The form of appraisal method would include Class A, B, or C and the procedures for applying the method.

For large, critical system source selections, rigor in the results is paramount, and the SCAMPI A appraisal method might be employed. Other, less intrusive, methods are possible, especially when all the offerors are pursuing internal process improvement using CMMI models. These methods can range from simply reviewing the offerors' most recent internal appraisal results (which is not recommended), to performing Class B or C appraisals on selected process areas critical to the procurement. Innovative methods of appraisal of CMMI processes have included a technique where offerors reported their own CMMI appraisal results to the government team as part of their proposal. The government team determined the process areas that were critical to the effort and identified risks for each offeror based on the reported appraisal results. Teams then visited each site, verifying selected portions of the offeror's processes and analyzing the offeror's responses to the risk items.

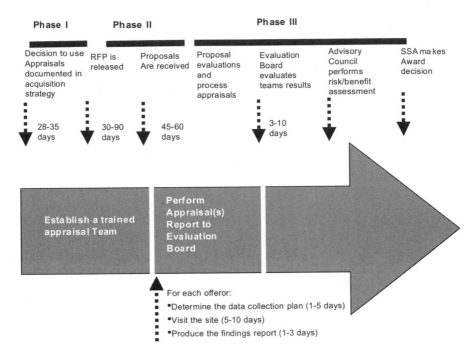

Figure 6-1: *Timeline for a Source Selection Appraisal*

Also, specific objectives for the appraisal must be determined. These include

- Determining discriminators between offerors to support source selection
- Identifying risks in process performance that might affect contract performance
- Obtaining contractual commitment to use mature processes
- Satisfying policy or regulations applicable to the sponsoring acquisition organization
- Addressing post-contract follow-on process improvement actions

Constraints on the appraisal have to be considered early during the planning phase and may be revisited often during planning. These include

- **Cost and schedule constraints.** Both for the sponsoring organization and the contractor organization(s) undergoing appraisal. Sponsoring organization costs include personnel effort, travel, and training. These costs will be affected by appraisal scope, number of offerors, and locations of the appraisal. Costs for the offerors are typically assumed by the appraised organization; however, there may be circumstances where the costs will be charged to the contract.

- **Discussion constraints.** Decisions must be made regarding whether performing a SCAMPI appraisal will constitute discussions for the source selection. The contracting officer or a legal or procurement official must make this decision.

- **Placement in the Evaluation Board structure.** If the appraisal team is part of the board, there may be constraints on team membership, such as government employees only.

- **Reporting constraints.** What can be reported to the appraised organization for preliminary and final findings and when they can be presented must be determined during planning. It is important to work with the contracting officer to determine these constraints. Note that for a SCAMPI A appraisal, at a minimum, summary strengths and weaknesses for each appraised process area must be presented to both the appraised organization and the sponsor. For the sponsor, other reporting requirements (maturity level, capability level, color ratings, goal satisfaction, and strengths and weaknesses) must be negotiated with the sponsor.

In summary, the planning phase for the use of SCAMPI in source selection requires many decisions to be made (and probably remade). Section 6.2 is an excerpt of the *SCAMPI Version 1.1 Method Implementation Guidance for Government Source Selection and Contract Process Monitoring Handbook* (SCAMPI MIG) (CMU/SEI-2002-HB-002), which should be consulted and understood prior to embarking on using SCAMPI for source selection on a major system.

6.3 The Appraisal Team

There are a few team considerations for external appraisals that are different from internal appraisals, but team expertise and training requirements are the same except that the team lead must be familiar with the considerations and constraints described at the beginning of this chapter. Managing these constraints is a major part of the team lead's responsibilities. When working on a source selection, the team lead should not only be an SEI authorized Lead Appraiser but should have experience in preparing for and conducting source selections.

The relationship of the SCAMPI team and the Evaluation Board is an aspect of SCAMPI external appraisals that is different from internal use. There are three common placements for the SCAMPI appraisal results—as part of the Technical Evaluation, as part of the Management Evaluation, and as part of the Past Performance Evaluation. The choice is dependent on the acquisition organization's policies and the sponsor's preferences; however, the SCAMPI appraisal should be placed so that it is a significant consideration in the source selection evaluation, commensurate with the degree of risk immature software and systems engineering processes have on program success. In addition, the relationship of the SCAMPI team and the Evaluation Board has implications for the team and its members. If the SCAMPI team is a member of the board, it may have more influence on the source selection results; however, all team members may have to meet board membership requirements, for example, they may all have to be government employees. This could severely limit the availability of trained team members, especially SCAMPI lead appraisers. If the SCAMPI team is an advisor to the Evaluation Board, the team may employ employees of *Federally Funded Research and Development Centers* (FFRDCs) and other contract employees. Another option is for the sponsoring organization to outsource the SCAMPI appraisals to SEI-licensed SCAMPI Appraiser companies.

Another consideration for the SCAMPI appraisal is whether to use multiple appraisal teams. In the instance of several bidders on a major acquisition, multiple appraisal teams may be necessary considering the severe time constraints of a typical acquisition. In this case, not only must each team have equivalent expertise and training and be lead by a SCAMPI Lead Appraiser, but also some sort of quality control of results should be instituted. One successful method used in a past procurement action was for the team leads to meet and review their results and data for each appraisal.

6.4 Issues for External Appraisals

This section discusses some issues for external appraisals that are different from internal appraisals. These issues may be for both source selection and for contract process monitoring.

6.4.1 Source Selection

In a source selection situation, model representation (staged or continuous) and scope (process areas, maturity level, and capability level) are chosen by the acquirer, possibly after receiving comments from offerors via draft RFPs. These choices must be made considering the risk and complexity of the system under development, the anticipated contractual environment (single developer, teaming, or subcontracting) and the anticipated experience and maturity of the potential offerors.

For a large, high risk, unprecedented software-intensive system, a high level of maturity in both software and systems engineering for development team members may be desired. For a relatively small effort with offerors limited to a known group with special expertise, a quick look at process areas critical to the development might suffice.

When the acquisition is with one supplier with no subcontractors, the processes appraised might not include Supplier Agreement Management or Integrated Supplier Management. Conversely, if the acquisition involves many subcontractors, special emphasis should be placed on these supplier process areas. If the effort involves integrated teams with members from contractors, subcontractors, and/or the government, the IPPD process areas should be included in the appraisals.

If the offerors are expected to be the major government systems integrators and developers and the effort is major, a high degree of maturity and/or capability should be expected. If the field will be a mixed bag of large, small, government, and commercial bidders, either a lower maturity/capability level expectation or a tailored approach might be used. It might be feasible to require adequate performance (capability level 2) in a few critical management process areas and reward higher performance in others deemed important to the development.

In any case, decisions about the model and appraisal method used in a source selection activity must be made early, communicated to all potential bidders, and strenuously adhered to during the source selection. The alternative to this is to have a strong legal team ready and able to defend the acquisition organization in the inevitable protest actions that will follow.

6.4.2 Contract Process Monitoring

After contract award, SCAMPI appraisals can be used to mitigate risks identified during source selection, incentivize process improvement during the contract period, and track actual versus planned improvement activities. The spectrum of use ranges from formal appraisals similar to those used in source selections to the types of appraisals used during internal process improvement. The ideal situation, of course, is where the contractor and sponsor (typically the acquisition organization) work as a team to improve processes of both parties. CMMI then becomes the common basis for the improvement, providing a common language for describing processes and a common yardstick for measuring their state.

When used for contract process monitoring, the contractual vehicle is used to provide contractual incentive, describing the sponsoring organization's goals and the method for evaluating progress. The sponsoring organization and the contractor jointly agree to the criteria and approach and establish mechanisms, such as award fee increments, to reward progress. Appraisals are used, typically with a Class B or C method to measure progress after an initial baseline is established. After the baseline appraisal, the findings are provided to the contractor; the contractor uses the findings to plan improvement actions, and the sponsor and contractor jointly agree on the plan. Appraisals are then used to measure progress against the improvement plan.

The model and appraisal method class used in contract process monitoring are typically defined by consensus of both the sponsor and contractor and might reflect areas judged weak during the baseline appraisal. In later appraisals, teams might just look at areas with weaknesses or could start on new areas as defined in the process improvement plan.

In a team situation, these appraisals might be for internal improvement with the added participation of the sponsor's organization or they could have a more external flavor. This depends on the view of the sponsor of the contractor's responsiveness and past progress. Ideally, the sponsor and contractor view this as a means to improve performance and productivity for both parties; thus, the external appraisals would be like the internal ones. However, life is not always roses; the sponsor and contractor may not agree on how process improvement is progressing, and the appraisal may be used as more of an audit.

In any case, use of SCAMPI for contract process monitoring should be planned prior to contract award and should be enabled in the contract and agreed to by both parties. This planning might not be as detailed as that required for use in source selection, but the details of how to incentivize process improvement on (potentially) the part of both the contractor and sponsor requires careful thought based on past experience and the current environment. We have seen many times the unintended consequences of incentivizing what is thought to be improved performance, but turns out otherwise. One case would be our Friday night softball league team. Jim Armstrong, the coach, decided we needed better defense and focused on the objective of improving our capability to perform double plays. He awarded a case of beer after each game for an improvement on the number of double plays. The team's response, after much thought and debate, was for the pitcher to walk the first batter every inning to provide the opportunity for more double plays.

Part III

Using SCAMPI

Now that the meal is over, you are ready to toast the chef, wish everyone good health, and sit back to engage in relaxing conversation. You may wish to reflect on how the food tasted, whether it met your expectations, and whether you might come back another time. In a similar vein, now that you are full with SCAMPI, no doubt you have lingering questions on nuances of the method and how its use can be value-added for your organization. So we close by exploring issues and suggesting ways in which SCAMPI appraisals could become a regular part of your process improvement diet.

Part III Contents

Chapter 7. SCAMPI Implementation Issues

We conclude with reflections on issues that those who conduct or undergo SCAMPI appraisals are likely to confront, both during the appraisals and after as they plan process improvements.

Chapter 7

SCAMPI Implementation Issues

su·shi scam·pi   an appraisal whose results seem fishy

mad cow scam·pi   an appraisal after which it is in
the team that needs to be institutionalized

Having laid the foundation with a full presentation of SCAMPI, Part III, "Using SCAMPI," concludes with discussion of various issues related to appraisals and process improvement. How are appraisals of most benefit to an organization just starting process improvement, as opposed to a (so-called) high-maturity organization? How are appraisals best conducted across various disciplines, such as software, systems engineering, and (perhaps) hardware engineering? How does an organization comply with a CMMI model and conduct a successful SCAMPI appraisal and at the same time meet the requirements of other standards, quality initiatives, and customer-driven needs?

In reading this section, the reader should keep in mind four important considerations that shape the discussion. First, the SCAMPI method is relatively new; thus, the material in this section should be viewed as a work in progress. Second, the SCAMPI method is model-sensitive. That is, the SCAMPI method helps an organization to gain insight into its process area capability or organizational maturity by identifying the strengths and weaknesses of its current processes. It does this relative to the CMMI model representations and not factors outside of the models. This does not mean that the SCAMPI method and the associated models are not extensible, but that the models are the basis for the appraisals. Steps should be taken prior to the appraisal to define any factors to be assessed from outside the current models.

Third, the SCAMPI method is a diagnostic tool that supports, enables, and encourages an organization's commitment to process improvement. By itself, the SCAMPI method does not provide the commitment. The commitment is nominally based on business objectives of the organization being appraised; thus, it is important that the sponsor and the appraisal team both clearly understand why the organization is undertaking the SCAMPI and the anticipated returns. Fourth, the SCAMPI method is also the standard benchmarking tool for CMMI process area capability and maturity level profiles. At a 2,000-foot level, the rationale for systematic process improvement is international in scope. Firms improve their processes to become more competitive in the marketplace with the expectation that effective and efficient processes increase quality and productivity and reduce risk and cost. Although there are risks associated with using a model for systematic process improvement, the CMM for Software has been very successful all over the world; it is reasonable to assume that CMMI will also be effective in improving the bottom line of business. The question the customer often asks to mitigate risk is "to what extent do I want to do business with a low-maturity versus a high-maturity organization?" Given the demonstrated benefits of high-maturity processes, the SCAMPI method is an effective standard benchmarking tool that can be used by the developer, among other things, as a market discriminator.

7.1 Deploying CMMI-Compliant Processes

Within the CMMI models, the Process Management category of process areas contains the fundamental practices that are necessary to create and improve processes. One challenge for organizations is how to define a process to develop and deploy its standard processes. There are other process improvement models that use the same basic approach as that found in CMMI. IDEAL is one such model; we discuss it here to relate how it can be used to create and deploy standard processes that meet the intent of the CMMI. IDEAL is available from the Software Engineering Institute; see http://sei.cmu.edu/ideal.

IDEAL has five basic steps, as shown in Figure 7-1.

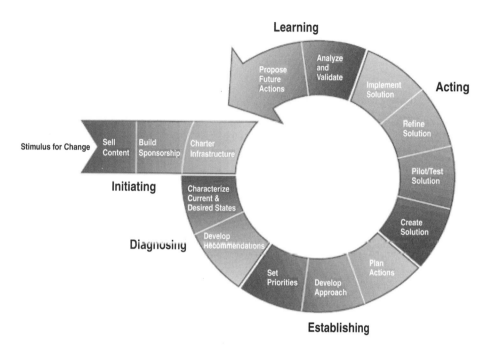

Figure 7-1: *The IDEAL Model*

7.1.1 Initiating Phase

Some event or stimulus for change initiates the process improvement activities. In OPF, Specific Practice 1.1-1, "Establish Organizational Process Needs," covers this. The process needs and objectives are the key drivers for the creation and improvement of processes. It is critical for an organization to identify these needs and objectives prior to developing processes. When this step is not performed, the processes are more difficult to deploy to the people in the organization. The needs and objectives give the people the motivation for changing the environment in which they work. When the objectives do not relate to the specifics of the organization's primary goals, the changes more than likely will not be successful. For example, if the objective is to achieve CMMI maturity level 3, the employees will be thinking, "Here we go again with more of this non-value-added stuff we have to do." But if the objectives relate to improving specific things the people are doing and they can relate the improvements to getting products out the door faster or with less expense, they will accept the new or improved processes with much less resistance to change.

This makes the Initiating phase critical to the overall success of the process improvement effort. The context must be set so the people can relate the change to their success, sponsorship must be built to provide the organization with the commitment necessary for change, and the infrastructure needed to complete the improvements must be established.

7.1.2 Diagnosing Phase

The Diagnosing phase relates to OPF Specific Practice 1.2-1, "Appraise the Organization's Processes." In this phase, the current processes and situation are compared to the businesses needs and objectives. This could be performed with a CMMI appraisal as well as other model appraisals, or it could be a simple analysis of the current situation against the needs and objectives. The key output of this activity is to determine the weaknesses and strengths of the current situation compared to the organization's process needs and objectives.

7.1.3 Establishing Phase

The characterization of the current situation produces a set of recommendations for improvement. These recommendations are then implemented during the Establishing phase of the IDEAL model. This step is covered by OPF Specific Practice 1.3-1, "Identify the Organization's Process Improvements," and Specific Practice 2.1-1, "Establish Process Action Plans."

The first step in the Establishing phase is to establish priorities for the improvement recommendations. Several factors are involved in determining the priorities, such as impact, resources available, dependencies between possible actions, and satisfaction of business goals and objectives. After the priorities are set, the approach should be developed for the improvement recommendations. The characterization information, recommendations, priorities, and approach provide the information needed to plan the actions for process improvement.

7.1.4 Acting Phase

The Acting phase executes the plans. OPF addresses this phase with Specific Practice 2.2-1, "Implement Process Action Plans," and Specific Practice 2.3-1, "Deploy Organizational Process Assets." First, a potential solution is developed according to the plan and the solution is tested either by piloting, peer analysis, or some other method. The test by piloting is probably the most informative way to evaluate process improvements. The process can then be refined prior to deploying it to the entire organization. When the improved process is determined to be ready for deployment, it is then implemented across the organization.

7.1.5 Learning Phase

The Learning phase ensures that the processes deployed across the organization are effective and meet the organization's business needs and objectives. OPF Specific Practice 2.4-1, "Incorporate Process-Related Experiences into the Organization's Process Assets," covers this phase of the IDEAL model. The Analyze and Validate step provides the continuous improvement features of the overall process improvement program. This information is used in the Propose Future Actions step and links the improvement activities back to the first phase to help the organization determine when change is necessary.

Thus we see that the IDEAL model supports the CMMI Organizational Process Improvement process area very well. In fact, as the organization moves up the maturity level in performance, the practices associated with Organizational Process Performance and Organizational Innovation and Deployment can be integrated into these same five phases very easily. The basic process addressed by OPF is improved to enhance the execution of these phases. As an example, one of the IDEAL steps is to Pilot/Test the Solution. Piloting is actually addressed by OID Specific Practice Pilot Improvements.

Using the Engineering PAs for Process Improvement

In CMMI, product development processes are modeled by the Engineering process areas. These process areas focus on products and product components. The definition of product includes processes. Why do organizations develop separate processes for developing deliverable products and processes? To illustrate how the same development process can be used for hardware, software, services, and processes we will examine the relationship between the Engineering process areas and the IDEAL model. We have already seen how the IDEAL model relates to OPF.

The Initiating phase relates to *Requirements Development* (RD) Specific Goal 1 where needs are elicited and high level requirements are generated. Specific Goal 3 addresses the analysis and validation of the requirements. This is the same function described in setting the content for PI, building sponsorship, and chartering the infrastructure steps in this phase.

The Diagnosing phase is closely related to the RD and *Technical Solution* (TS) Specific Goal 1, where alternative solutions are developed and analyzed to ensure that the right product is being developed. As recommended in the Engineering process areas, Validation and Verification activities should be performed throughout the development process. This is the same in the IDEAL model, as we have described.

The Establishing phase is closely related to TS Specific Goal 2 where the selected solutions are designed, verified, and validated. There may also be some integration issues between processes that have to be designed and evaluated. Buying or developing tools to support the processes must be addressed, as in TS and maybe Supplier Agreement Management.

The Acting phase relates to TS Specific Goal 3 where implementation is performed, as well as Product Integration, Verification, and Validation process area activities.

The Learning phase is also closely related to Validation activities. It also relates to the monitor and controlling practices in CMMI.

The organization probably invests a lot of effort into creating a robust product development process. It should consider creating tailoring guidelines for this process when developing its process improvement process.

7.2 Objective Evidence

Objective evidence is the single most critical aspect of an appraisal. As discussed in Chapter 2, "New Aspects of the SCAMPI Method," SCAMPI is a verification appraisal method rather than a discovery method. That means the organization is responsible for providing objective evidence to show that its processes satisfy the practices and goals of the model so the appraisal team can verify implementation of the model. The model has some hints on what objective evidence could be provided for each practice. The practice statement implies that there are work products generated by having a process task that satisfies the practice. For example, Requirements Management SP 1.4-2 states the following: *"Maintain bidirectional traceability among the requirements and the project plans and work products."* One would expect to see a traceability report that shows bidirectional traces. Typical work products can give us hints on what could be shown to an appraisal team too. The following is an example from the same practice:

Typical Work Products

- Requirements traceability matrix [PA146.IG101.SP104.W101]
- Requirements tracking system [PA146.IG101.SP104.W102]

Other practices in the model may not present such a clear idea of what would be objective evidence, though. How can we be reasonably sure that we have interpreted the model correctly—the same way the appraisal team will interpret it?

Another factor in an appraisal is that the team will be looking for three types of evidence:

- Direct Evidence
- Indirect Evidence
- Affirmations

Now, you may ask with good reason, "Why am I now learning about different types of evidence that are not described in the model?" The Appraisal Method Expert Team created PIIDs to help organizations and appraisers know the type of evidence to generate from the processes and what to look for during an appraisal for each practice. These documents give further hints on what may be used as objective evidence. Keep in mind that these are only possible work products generated by processes that could satisfy the evidence requirements in an appraisal—your processes define exactly what work products are produced. You must provide the trace of these work products to the model so that an appraisal team can *verify* that the processes satisfy the model.

So, what are these PIIDs, and why haven't you seen them before? The fundamental idea of practice implementation indicators is based on the presumption that the conduct of an activity or the implementation of a practice will result in evidence that is attributable to the practice. Table 7-1 shows the PIID for the same practice; REQM, Specific Practice 1.4-2.

Each PIID lists the goal statement and the practice statement for reference. It then shows the example direct, indirect, and affirmations for that practice. Notice that the PIID also lists the traceability matrix or report as direct evidence. But what about the indirect evidence? It lists several things that could be used to show that this practice is being executed. Most PIIDs do not list anything for the affirmations.

The next section of the PIID shows some appraisal considerations. These are guidance, interpretation, or discussion targeted to assessors. Of course, if the organization knows what the appraisers are looking for it helps them prepare for an appraisal.

You're the team that can use this block to document the processes' work products or artifacts—things that are produced by each program.

The next section, Appraisal Team Notes, would be used in the appraisal to document the team's notes about each practice and would be used in the findings generation activity.

The PIIDs are located on the SEI Web site. The AMET did not create PIIDs for every PA in the model. Appendix B, "Practice Implementation Indicator Descriptions," contains the direct and indirect evidence indicators that the authors created for each of the process areas.

So now that you know what PIIDs are, how do you use them? The recommended way to use PIIDs is to consider the direct and indirect work products when you are generating your objective evidence mappings to the model. You should also use the model, especially the practice statements, typical work products, and notes to decide what best represents your processes. Do not rely only on PIIDs, practice statements, or typical work products either. Keep in mind that your processes are designed to work for you and your organization. The work products they produce should support your business goals and objectives first.

Table 7-1: *REQM SP 1.4-2 PIID*

Goal ID	REQM SG 1 Requirements are managed and inconsistencies with project plans and work products are identified.
Practice ID	REQM SP 1.4-2 *Maintain bi-directional traceability among the requirements and the project plans and work products.*
PII Type	Example Direct Artifacts	Example Indirect Artifacts	Affirmations
Example Evidence (Look Fors / Listen Fors)	[1. Requirements traceability matrix] • Reports or database indicating traceability of requirements to/from project plans and work products, at each applicable level of system decomposition.	[2. Requirements tracking system] • Criteria and completed checklists and minutes for review of requirements traceability. • Requirements tracking logs. • Revision and maintenance of requirements traceability across the life cycle. • Listings of allocated requirements included in reviews of project plans and work products across the life cycle. • Requirements mappings used to support impact appraisals.	

(continued)

Table 7-1: *Continued*

Appraisal Considerations	• Ensure that both vertical and horizontal traceability are included (e.g., across functions and/or interfaces) • (How do we assess traceability of requirements to "project plans"? This is probably more implicit than explicit, and applies to plans such as test plans, V&V plans, etc. See PP PA for project plans that might be affected. The appraisal team must reach consensus on how this is to be assessed for the organization.) NO – How does the project go forward if the requirements are not driving the project tasks and activities?
Organizational Implementation Evidence	
Appraisal Team Notes	

7.3 Appraisal Strategies Across Disciplines

The SCAMPI appraisal method is generally specified to be applicable regardless of the CMMI model and disciplines being appraised. Some distinctions in the method are applied, such as ensuring representation of discipline expertise among the appraisal team members and selection of participants from the organizational unit. This section describes some of the issues that must be addressed to ensure coverage of appropriate disciplines when considering implementation of model practices.

Coverage is a measure of the extent of examination (such as software, systems, integrated product development processes, and so on) of what the organization does and how it performs its work. Coverage of appropriate disciplines is largely determined by how an organization does its work. Business objectives drive selected parts of the organization's objectives to be selected because the organizational structures are aligned to best meet their business objectives. The coverage "goodness" is tied back to the business objectives.

One issue is that different organizational structures often provide suggestions on how the CMMI may be interpreted, which can have a direct impact on the coverage associated with the SCAMPI appraisal. For example, business objectives can result in organizational structures that support small project teams, short-duration projects, geographically dispersed organizations, maintenance organizations, component-based development projects, in-house development projects, and so on. If the CMMI approach is tailored to accommodate the way the workflow is accomplished in different types of organizational structures, the appraisal needs to take this tailoring into consideration. Given that the organizational coverage of the CMMI initiative is understood, we are now in position to address the discipline of coverage.

Figure 7-2 demonstrates a context for discipline coverage in three dimensions: process, capability, and performance. Process capability is a good indicator of the organizational process improvement experience and the number of disciplines involved in process improvement. As the organization improves its systematic process improvement activities and more process areas are involved, organizational integration of the workflow processes become more important. The resultant improved workflow processes involve more of the organization, thus extending the coverage required for the SCAMPI appraisal. Measurement also becomes more important in the decision processes as the organization improves its process maturity.

Another issue being addressed for either the staged or continuous representation is the following: Should an organization be assessed for a process area that it is not used in the performance of its workflow processes? The resolution of this question is mostly on a case-by-case basis.

The staged model representation fixes the number and type of process areas to be addressed for a given maturity level. In general, discipline coverage becomes more important and complex at higher levels of process maturity. Higher levels of maturity require the involvement of more disciplines given that the number of different process areas being appraised increases. Furthermore, at the higher levels of maturity, statistical and other process measurement mechanisms often enhance the interaction of different disciplines. The SCAMPI appraisal is more intense relative to discipline interaction at the higher versus lower levels of maturity. An issue at higher levels of maturity is determining how the process areas interact relative to the workflow of the organization. The continuous model representation permits the selection of process areas that affect the disciplines involved. One issue is understanding the organization's workflow process and goals in sufficient detail to determine if the right process areas and associated disciplines have been selected.

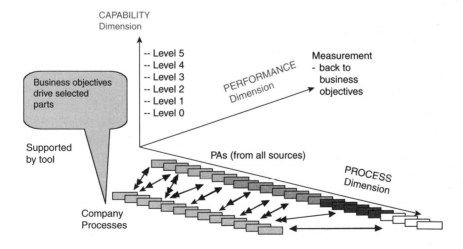

Figure 7-2: *Context for Discipline Coverage*

A key to appropriate discipline coverage across dimensions of capability, process, and measurement is an understanding of the business issues, process integration, and stakeholder involvement and expectations. In this context, shareholder involvement covers all aspects of business issues associated with organizational, engineering, and program processes and integration. The next few paragraphs address this subject.

Because SCAMPI is an appraisal method that measures the organization's processes against the CMMI model, the model probably will not map exactly to some of the organizational, engineering, and program business issues facing the organization. The challenge at the organizational level is to obtain a clear understanding of how the SCAMPI appraisal effectively addresses the meaning of the term "integration" relative to organizational goals. For example, at the organizational level there is often a business objective to define and integrate the processes and interfaces between different organizational entities of the total enterprise (such as engineering, manufacturing, marketing, quality, sales, HR, and so on) so that the organization can cut costs and improve productivity. Unfortunately, many of the organizational processes in today's organizations are stovepipes versus being integrated with one another. As a result, there may be confusion on who owns a particular CMMI practice and how that practice can be satisfied in the most effective manner. The challenge at the engineering level is how to obtain a clear understanding of how the appraisal effectively addresses the meaning of the term "integration" relative to the engineering goals. Engineering addresses a set of interdisciplinary activities leading to a software-intensive system that works and meets the stakeholder needs. The engineering function interfaces with most of the organizational entities. A key issue is often the lack of interface definition between engineering and the other organizational entities. For example, there may be confusion on the type and amount of data that needs to be generated at these interface points to satisfy a specific practice. The challenge at the program level is how to obtain a clear understanding of how the appraisal effectively addresses the meaning of the term "integration" relative to program goals. A key issue is often the extent that the selected programs for the SCAMPI appraisal cover the entire acquisition life cycle. For example, new starts are not in position to provide evidence that down stream processes have been executed, and legacy programs are often not in position to demonstrate new processes.

Another major consideration is the stakeholder (and any associated work products). The issues include selecting the appropriate stakeholders and ensuring that appropriate work products are available to demonstrate that the processes are being followed. An issue associated with the SCAMPI appraisal versus a CBA IPI appraisal is the shift to a focus on verification versus discovery. In general, the SCAMPI Readiness Review objective is targeted at making sure the information is available for the SCAMPI appraisal team and that there is limited effort for the discovery of new information. This focus on verification versus discovery places a special emphasis on identifying the appropriate stakeholders and associated work products that verify the processes being assessed. The challenge is how to select the appropriate participants who can cover what the organization does and how it performs its work over the process areas being appraised. CMMI has a requirement to identify and involve relevant stakeholders, execute and monitor the plan for stakeholder involvement, and take corrective action to address the causes for lack of involvement, as appropriate. According to CMMI, a stakeholder is "a group or individual that is affected by or in some way accountable for the outcome of an undertaking. Stakeholders may include project members, suppliers, customers, end users, and others." The key focus is on the CMMI definition of "relevant stakeholders," selected stakeholders who should participate in various activities of the process. These stakeholders could participate in one or more of the following capacities: planning, decision making, communicating, coordinating with groups outside the project, reviewing work products, participating in process appraisals, providing stakeholder needs with regard to the process or project, participating in requirements validation, and helping to resolve problems and issues.

7.4 Initial Process Improvement Efforts

When an organization is in the early stages of integrated process improvement, what special considerations are important when implementing CMMI and conducting CMMI appraisals? Getting started can have its challenges for reasons discussed in this section. This section addresses the concerns and issues that are most commonly raised by organizations in the early stages of integrated process improvement. Much of the material presented here is the result of lessons learned by the Software Productivity Consortium in assisting a very large number of organizations reach their systematic process improvement goals. The best time to address these concerns is in about four to five years when we have more information related to issues facing organizations using CMMI; thus, at this time, the issues provided here comprise a representative set of issues.

- **Complexity:** One of the challenges is to understand the "language" of CMMI given that the context of the statements may not be immediately obvious. The authors of the CMMI models incorporated lessons learned from the source models to make CMMI applicable to a broader set of organizations than any of the source models are. Whereas the SW-CMM was based on implementation of a specified set of software Key Process Areas, the EIA 731 model was based on an organization's selection of applicable focus areas. CMMI merged these two concepts by creating a staged representation of the model that is familiar to software organizations and a continuous representation that is comparable to systems organizations. The dual representations allow organizations to follow a prescribed implementation of the CMMI process areas (staged representation) or a selected implementation of CMMI process areas (continuous representation). All organizations will discover some overlap and interdependence among the practices and even process areas. As with the source models, organizations that do not perform traditional full life-cycle engineering development may struggle to understand the relevance of all the CMMI process areas and practices in their environments. Even the terminology used in CMMI may initially be viewed as "not applicable to my environment."

  Small organizations that found the source models to be overwhelming from a size perspective find CMMI to be even larger and more complex. For these organizations, a roadmap through the sheer volume of process areas and practices is needed.

  Organizations that are moving to more "agile" methodologies may initially view the CMMI requirements as being in direct opposition to the objectives and practices of their methodologies. For these organizations, understanding how to interpret the numerous practices of CMMI is important.

  As a result of the previous comments, the appraisal approach needs to take into consideration the context of the appraisal, including the business drivers, organization focus, life-cycle deliver framework, and other elements of the organization environment.

- **Size:** Whether your organization is experienced in process improvement or not, an organization may be overwhelmed by the size and complexity of the CMMI model and associated SCAMPI. With over 700 pages of guidance in each of the two representations (continuous and staged) and multiple disciplines to mix and match, making sense of CMMI can seem daunting. However, with greater familiarity with CMMI, you will come to appreciate its contents as added value.

  CMMI is large for several important reasons. As an integration of three source models, CMMI SE/SW/IPPD/SS has many more practices than any of the source models have. For example, a total of 494 specific and generic practices in the staged representation versus 316 key practices for the SW CMM staged model.

  CMMI with all extensions (the CMMI SE/SW/IPPD/SS) has 25 process areas, more than any of the source models have. It provides more process guidance across the entire development life cycle than any of the source models.

  The structure of a CMMI process area is more comprehensive than that of the source models. As a result, the CMMI process areas typically have more practices than process areas of the source models.

  The informative material of CMMI is more extensive than that of any of the source models.

  After becoming very familiar with CMMI, if its size is still an obstacle for using it in an organization, the organization may create an interpreted CMMI that is significantly smaller and has specific meaning to it.

  Given the size of both the CMMI and SCAMPI description (for example, the Standard CMM Appraisal Method for Process Improvement [SCAMPI] Version 1.1: Method Definition Document [MDD] is over 200 pages), the appraisal team should, at a minimum, provide an executive summary about what SCAMPI is and its associated roles and responsibilities. For the key stakeholders, a model overview of SCAMPI that provides a more extensive coverage is often appropriate (for example, every prospective appraisal team member is expected to read a large section of the MDD).

- **Applicability of Certain Process Areas and Practices:** Based on current work methods, some organizations have difficulty seeing the applicability of some CMMI process areas and practices to its environments. It may be tempting to dismiss these process areas or practices as not applicable. Chapter 6 of the CMMI staged representation indicates that a process area can be excluded if it is "not applicable." The use of the term "not applicable" is further defined to mean "not within the organization's scope of work." In these cases, an organization can receive a maturity level that indicates which process areas are not applicable.

One organization tried to use the argument that PPQA was not applicable to its organization because its customer would not fund it. The appraisal team correctly determined that this process area was applicable to the organization and therefore needed to be satisfied in order to receive a CMMI maturity level 2 rating. The CMMI author team intended exclusions to apply to organizations where the process area was truly outside the scope of the organization's work. The typical example is SAM for organizations that have no suppliers of products or services external to the organization that are critical to the development effort.

In most cases, the challenge as an organization is to understand how to develop value-added implementations of previously unperformed processes or practices. Of course, any organization can choose to use the continuous representation and select specific process areas to include in its process area profile. This way, the organization can focus on process areas and practice areas that best suit its business needs and resources. This is an appropriate response for organizations that do not need maturity ratings but are looking for capability ratings for specific process areas.

7.5 Overlaps in CMMI

The process areas, specific practices, and generic practices in the CMMI are not mutually exclusive. You will find both overlap and dependencies among these components. Specific overlaps and dependencies include

- **Specific Practice and Generic Practice Overlap:** An example of this is Generic Practice 2.7, "Manage Configurations and the Configuration Management Process Area." Organizations that have already implemented and institutionalized the Configuration Management process area for all CMMI maturity level 2 process areas will find that they have already satisfied Generic Practice 2.7 for each of the maturity level 2 process areas. However, some specific practices that seem to be redundant to generic practices are actually different. For example, PP SP 2.4-1, "Plan for Project Resources," seems to overlap the generic practice GP 2.3, "Provide Resources." A close examination reveals that the practices are related but not redundant. For example, PP SP 2.4-1 creates the plan for resource usage; however, GP 2.3 requires the implementation or execution of the plan in order to be satisfied.

- **Base and Advanced Practices:** The engineering process areas in the continuous model contain both base and advanced practices. In some cases, the advanced practices build on the base practices. The base practices can be recognized by the suffix of "1" after the practice number. For example, RD Specific Practice 1.1-2, "Elicit Needs," is an advanced practice that builds on the base practice RD Specific Practice 1.1-1, "Collect Stakeholder Needs." In other cases, the advanced practice does not build on base practice but refers to an advanced practice (capability level 2 or higher). An example of this is TS Specific Practice 2.4-3, "Perform Make, Buy, or Reuse Analyses," which is a capability level 3 advanced practice.

- **Basic and Advanced Process Areas:** Each of the four process area categories (Process Management, Project Management, Engineering, and Support) contains both basic and advanced process areas. For example, in the Support category, the CM, PPQA, and MA are considered basic process areas while DAR, CAR, and OEI are considered advanced process areas.

- **Process Area Dependencies:** Although the process areas have been divided into four categories, there are dependencies among some of the process areas. For example, DAR, which is a support process area, describes specific practices that address the formal evaluations that are used in TS for selecting a technical solution and ISM for selecting a supplier.

The overlaps and interdependencies are often confusing to the novice reader of the CMMI, and may make CMMI appear more complex than it really is. The remedy for this confusion is to study Chapters 2-6 of CMMI carefully.

7.6 Importance of Documentation

CMMI makes greater documentation demands than do the source models. For example, GP 2.2, "Plan the Process for PAs," requires that processes be established and maintained. In Chapter 3 of CMMI, "established and maintained" is defined to mean documented and used. As a result, for capability levels or maturity level 2 or higher, essentially all processes must be documented and resultant artifacts captured for appraisal objective evidence.

It is important to recognize that such documentation is important to your organization, even without the threat of upcoming appraisals. Documented processes reduce or eliminate confusion about what should be done so that activities are performed more consistently. Recording what happens at reviews is important for being able to communicate the current state of affairs effectively throughout the organization and avoiding the confusion and rework of individuals or groups not getting the message about recent changes.

7.7 Appraisal Sponsor Considerations

There are different types of actors, so to speak, that are important to any systematic process improvement effort. These actors include the champion (often the CEO, COO, or equivalent government representative who has the vision and speaks for the organization), the sponsor (often the vice president of engineering or a significant division who has the vision, resources, and P/L authority for the effort), the change agent, and the individuals targeted to improve their processes. The sponsor is often the most important actor because he or she is the real source for establishing and maintaining organizational commitment.

One of the most important (and difficult) planning challenges is to establish realistic expectations with the appraisal sponsor. A key challenge is understanding the frame of reference of the sponsor. Often organizations that are just beginning their process improvement journey are sponsored by the engineering infrastructure organization, which can serve the internal or external needs of the organization. However, CMMI is often a wake-up call for organizations seeking to improve their integrated engineering enterprise, which in turn begins to involve more of the organization in a move to horizontally integrate functions, such as HR, Procurement, Finance, Manufacturing, and so on. As a result, the sponsor may change in the organization over time.

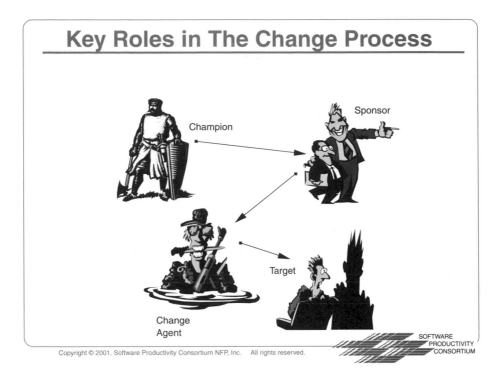

Figure 7-3: *Key Roles in the Change Process*

7.8 Roles in CMMI

Many of the practices in CMMI do not explicitly state the role of the individual or group that is expected to perform the activity. This allows maximum flexibility for assigning the responsibility for the activity. CMMI provides guidance in assigning roles to avoid conflict of responsibilities. For example, individuals performing QA are expected to be objective and CMMI states that "those performing QA activities should be separate from those directly involved in developing or maintaining the work product" (PPQA Introductory Notes). The lack of role definition can also be an issue given that the activity may not get done. One of the challenges is to ensure that activities can be appraised during the appraisal preparation process (for instance, that documentation is available to show that the activity is being done over an appropriate period of time to ensure institutionalization).

7.9 High Maturity Organizations

This section discusses the unique issues associated with the appraisal of high maturity organizations.

7.9.1 General

First, for organizations at level 3 and especially 4 and 5 maturity/capability, the business processes themselves are what should be rated rather than the process areas of the model. The rating process consists of two steps: verifying that the processes cover the base practices, and then rating the maturity of the processes.

At level 3, organizations have a standard process, which the projects tailor. The organization as a whole understands the importance of having and adhering to processes, and the staff is trained in all applicable processes. Management is better integrated across the organization. Measurements that are collected can be meaningfully compared across projects.

At level 4, organizations begin to manage key processes in a quantitative manner. They know what results their processes are expected to have, and they take action when the results show variations. Level 4 is achieved by collecting and analyzing enough measures about the subprocesses and their products that the organization understands what normal process behavior looks like and can take action when data indicates that something abnormal is happening.

At level 5, organizations continuously improve their processes. This includes seeking and eliminating root causes of product and process defects as well as incorporating new technology as appropriate. Level 5 is achieved by continuous improvement of the organization's standard processes according to lessons learned through causal analysis of defects. Clearly, both levels 4 and 5 in the continuous models apply principles in the same levels in the staged models.

7.9.2 Unique Appraisal Issues

- **High level of abstraction:** In order to be a CMMI model with very broad applicability, the models are, of necessity, quite abstract. As much as possible, the terminology in the CMMI is general, multipurpose, and neutral. This high level of abstraction permits application of the model to many diverse environments but can cause challenges with appraisals of organization at higher levels of maturity where limited experience is available. The appraisal team is required to seek an understanding of the business needs of the organization for which the appraisal is being requested. This understanding becomes more important at higher levels of maturity, in part due to the larger scope of the appraisal.

- **Need for socialization:** Usually, higher maturity efforts are comprised of more of the organization structure, more people, and more process owners. The need to socialize what CMMI and the SCAMPI appraisal process are and are not becomes very important to the success of the process improvement initiative. While an organization may recognize and seek help to address its challenges in using CMMI, the organization may not recognize its scope or intent of the CMMI/SCAMPI, and may proceed ignorantly down the wrong path.

- **CMMI is not a process or standard:** The SCAMPI appraisal approach enables an organization to gain insight into the organization's engineering capability to the extent it assesses the appropriate processes. CMMI is a model, not a process or standard. The model is a representation of reality, not reality itself. While the CMMI identifies the most important practices that must be present in a CMMI-compliant process, it does not address every activity that an organization performs to conduct its business effectively and which should be described in your processes. In many cases, an organization can identify processes that are important to its business but are not covered within the CMMI models (such as a human resource benefits process). This is especially true in high maturity organizations given the additional coverage of workflow processes compared to lower maturity organizations.

- **Organizational processes may not align with CMMI process areas:** An organization's processes usually evolve to satisfy business needs of the organization. An organization should *not* rewrite its processes to align with CMMI process areas. However, if an organization plans on measuring its processes in the context of CMMI, the goals of the CMMI model must be achieved. Thus, the appraisal must ensure that the organization has mapped processes to the CMMI practices to analyze how well processes address all CMMI requirements and expected elements for each goal. SCAMPI is designed to ensure these goals are met.

- **CMMI need not be implemented to the letter:** The CMMI does not require strict adherence "to the letter" of every practice. On the contrary, the CMMI states: " . . . organizations must use professional judgment to interpret CMMI practices. Although process areas depict behavior that should be exhibited in any organization, practices must be interpreted using an in-depth knowledge of the CMMI model being used, the organization, the business environment, and the specific circumstances involved." In higher maturity organizations, the workflow processes are often modified to improve performance and the appraisal must take this modification into account.

- **CMMI does apply to organizations that do not develop software or systems:** It is possible that an organization can be at a very high maturity and not develop software or systems; however, this does not mean that they are not doing engineering. The ability to appropriately assess these types of organizations can be difficult if not appropriately planned. Organizations that perform services, conduct research, or develop other types of deliverables may be actually performing engineering-like activities, such as transforming customer needs, expectations, and constraints into product solutions and supporting these product solutions throughout the life of the product. Indeed, CMMI provides extensive information relating to these practices. In addition, CMMI uses phrases such as "as appropriate" and "as necessary" to accommodate the needs of different organizations or projects.

  In cases where one or more process areas or practices are not applicable to an organizational business process and do not add value to the organization processes, an organization may consider using the continuous representation and focus on the process areas that are applicable to the organization. The organization may also need to identify alternative practices that contribute to goal satisfaction in a manner similar to the model practices.

- **CMMI may not be the only quality framework model an organization will ever need:** While CMMI addresses more processes than any previous source model, it still might not cover all processes that are performed in a business enterprise, nor does it have guidance for every type of business issue. Sometimes, other models, frameworks, standards, or methods are necessary to improve the effectiveness and efficiency of your organization or to meet your organizational business goals. Also, many organizations may be required by their customers to meet selected standards, such as ISO 9001:2000, to conform to other models (such as Six Sigma and Lean engineering). Often, a high-level maturity organization must conform to several standards and models but would like to limit the number of appraisals. As a result, the SCAMPI may be collecting information that can be used by other appraisal instruments.

- **Appraisal cost implications:** In general, higher-level capability/ maturity appraisals cost more because the number of process areas has increased. With up to 40% more practices between CMMI and the source models, for equivalent maturity and capability levels, CMMI appraisals tend to be longer and more costly. To control costs, the SCAMPI

  Focuses on process verification, putting more of a burden on an organization's preparation of objective evidence (direct and indirect artifacts and affirmation).

  Focuses less on discovery. This results in less hunting for evdence thus reducing the time of the appraisal.

  Costs will also be less if the enterprise has integrated processes across organizations, increasing the size and scope of the appraisal organization. If your organization has documented significant interpretation of the CMMI practices, provide these to the appraisal team in advance of the appraisal to reduce costs and increase accuracy of the appraisal.

- **Organizational structure of the Organizational Process Group:** Figure 7-4 provides a view of where the *Organization Process Group* (OPG) can be placed in the organization. In general, for high-level maturity organizations that are seeking to integrate their organizational quality management processes (such as Lean engineering, theory of constraints, Six Sigma, and CMMI), there is a push to move the OPG to high levels in the organization (such as from local to enterprise-wide).

• **Local,** Engineering, **or Enterprise-wide**
• **Separate, coordinated, or integrated at any level**

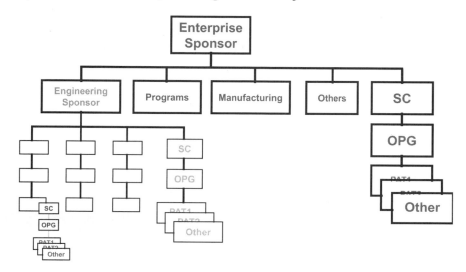

Figure 7-4: *Process Improvement Organization*

7.10 Tools

Some consideration of appraisal tools should be made by the organization. There are several tools available from suppliers that help prepare for and perform the appraisal. The following are some considerations or requirements that can be used for tool selection or development:

- Ability to hyperlink to all sources of documents
- Ability to add notes on practice instantiations by the programs
- Ability to add reviewer or verifier notes
- Ability to status instantiations
- Ability to capture appraiser mini-team comments
- Ability to capture appraisal team comments
- Ability to status each practice instantiation

- Ability to status each practice
- Ability to status each goal
- Ability to status each process area
- Ability to generate reports for multiple uses such as program, verifier, and appraisal team

An appraisal tool can provide information on the organization's PIIDs where it is needed most by the programs within the scope of the appraisal and by the appraisal team. Creating this information can help the organization evaluate its processes against the model. It can generate measures to help the organization understand its position and can help in planning for the appraisal as well as documenting appraisal results and providing information for process improvement.

Populating such a database can be expensive. Maintaining it might be difficult if the sources of the data are not controlled tightly too. But there are benefits that offset this cost. The primary benefit is that this database represents how processes are performed in the organization and can be used to train people, understand the implemented processes, and improve the processes.

7.11 Appraisal of a Multiorganization Program

The original concepts of the maturity models are based on the basic premise (or assumption) that a single organization "owns" the projects. The only exception to that would be some limited, albeit sometimes sizeable, subcontracts. In this instance, the programs can progress through independent process discipline at level 2, to tailoring and the use of the organization's standard set of processes at level 3. In most instances, this seems to work quite well.

This approach runs into problems with very large programs. Programs that cost billions of dollars and involve several large corporations don't fit this model. Even smaller programs that involve several divisions or business units of a major corporation have similar problems. The issue for SCAMPI comes when the customer or the lead organization decides that it wants the program to be appraised at some level. Similarly, if the organization wishes to claim an overall program level in a proposal based on individual ratings, there are conceptual problems.

To start with, such a program starts back at level 1, even if all the participants are at level 5. This is because there is no common process even at the program level. Participants will tailor their own organizational standard processes as part of their own level 3 or higher status. The likelihood that all these processes will be the same is slim to none.

There is, however, one solution. The lead organization must define an overall approach. The other participants then tailor their own standards to integrate with the program approach. The lead negotiates the interfaces to achieve a program approach while retaining the benefits of local process maturity.

When work can be divided cleanly, problems are reduced because the active interfaces are fewer between internal process steps. A more difficult situation is the integration of process on integrated product development teams where team members are proficient in conflicting processes.

Other issues arise when the program intends to operate at a level that is higher than the maturity of some of the participants. For those below level 3, this means starting with introducing the basic concepts of process maturity. Sometimes this means starting from scratch and can be quite painful. For level 4 or 5, the program must first define the measures that the program will use and integrate them with those that individual participants already use. In both cases, the lead organization is advised to assume a training role and be ready to mentor the less mature organizations until they are able to perform on their own.

The lead program should also establish a program process infrastructure and organization. This means having one or more sponsors, a steering committee across the organizations, and an integrated process group. These features should be proposed within the scope of the contract and be part of running the program if the approach is going to work.

The impact on a SCAMPI appraisal is multifaceted. The most important factor is that the appraisal team must understand that the usual meaning of organization, level, and tailoring will not directly apply. One of the hardest concepts to wrap the team's heads around will be the individual participant's use of different standard sources while still developing a common program approach. Basic concepts, such as top-level organizational policy, will be affected by the existence of both program policy and separate organizational policies that will apply at the same time and could conflict. However, with a little imagination on the part of the team, these problems can be resolved.

Another impact is the sheer size of the appraisal. It's not unusual to appraise organizations with multiple sites. Sometimes these are widely dispersed. In a large program, this will be even more of a challenge. Use of electronic communications aids in including multiple sites. However, some onsite presence may be required to fully understand how major players adapt their separate processes to reach a common approach. Separate appraisal efforts will be needed. The challenge is to integrate the results to reach an overall conclusion.

While there are new challenges in this application of SCAMPI, the problems are solvable. Several programs are successfully addressing this case. The real work is, as usual, in developing and implementing the program-wide process approach and maturity. After that is done, appraising is relatively easy—as usual.

The Recipe

Your SCAMPI appraisal has been completed, achieving the ratings for which you hoped, and you are getting ready for another round of process improvement activities. At such a time we advise you to hold a party for the process improvement team. Here is our suggested main dish!

Classic Shrimp Scampi

1–1/2 lb jumbo shrimp

8 T clarified butter

1/5 c olive oil

1/3 c dry white wine

4 T minced garlic

Salt, black and red pepper to taste

1/3 c parsley

1/3 c seasoned breadcrumbs (optional)

1/4 c Parmesan and Romano cheeses

Split the shrimp down the back, leaving the tail tip section of shell on the shrimp. Devein. Heat butter and olive oil over medium heat. Sauté minced garlic until soft, not brown. Add wine and shrimp. Cook until pink and firm, about 1–2 minutes on each side. Season with salt and pepper to taste. Sprinkle with parsley and cheeses. Add seasoned breadcrumbs (optional). Serve over linguine or basmati rice. Serves six people.

Appendix A

Glossary

accurate observation   An observation extracted from data collected during an appraisal that has been determined by the appraisal team to be (a) worded appropriately; (b) based on information seen or heard; (c) relevant to the appraisal reference model being used; (d) significant, such that it can be classified as a strength, weakness, or alternative practice; and (e) not redundant with other observations.

alternative practice   A practice that is a substitute for one or more generic or specific practices contained in the CMMI model that achieves an equivalent effect toward satisfying the goal associated with the model practices. Alternative practices are not necessarily one-for-one replacements for the generic or specific practices.

appraisal   An examination of one or more processes by a trained team of professionals using an appraisal reference model as the basis for determining, at a minimum, strengths and weaknesses.

appraisal action plan   A detailed plan to address an appraisal finding.

appraisal findings   (See "findings.")

appraisal input   The collection of appraisal information required before data collection can commence.

appraisal method class   Designation assigned to an appraisal method that satisfies a defined subset of requirements in the ARC (CMU/SEI-2001-TR-034). The three classes defined in the ARC align with typical applications of appraisal methods.

appraisal objectives   The desired outcome(s) established for an appraisal as derived from the business objectives of the appraisal sponsor.

appraisal output   All the tangible results from an appraisal. (See also "appraisal record.")

appraisal participants   Members of the organizational unit who participate in providing information during the appraisal.

appraisal rating   The value assigned by an appraisal team to (1) a CMMI goal or process area, (2) the capability level of a process area, or (3) the maturity level of an organizational unit. The rating is determined by enacting the defined rating process for the appraisal method being employed.

appraisal record   An orderly, documented collection of information that is pertinent to the appraisal and adds to the understanding and verification of the appraisal findings and ratings generated.

appraisal reference model   The model to which an appraisal team correlates implemented process activities.

appraisal scope   The definition of the boundaries of the appraisal encompassing the organizational limits and the CMMI model limits.

appraisal sponsor   The individual, internal or external to the organization being appraised, who requires the appraisal to be performed and provides financial or other resources to carry it out.

appraisal tailoring   Selection of options within the appraisal method for use in a specific instance. The intent of tailoring is to assist an organization in aligning application of the method with its business needs and objectives.

appraisal team leader   The person who leads the activities of an appraisal and has satisfied the qualification criteria for experience, knowledge, and skills defined by the appraisal method.

assessment   An appraisal that an organization does to and for itself for the purpose of process improvement.

capability evaluation   An appraisal by a trained team of professionals used as a discriminator for supplier selection, contract monitoring, or incentives. Evaluations are used to help decision makers make better acquisition decisions, improve subcontractor performance, and provide insight to a purchasing organization.

consensus   A method of decision making that allows team members to develop a common basis of understanding and develop general agreement concerning a decision that all team members are willing to support.

consolidation   The activity of collecting and summarizing the information provided during an appraisal into a manageable set of data to (a) determine the extent to which the data are corroborated and cover the areas being investigated, (b) determine the data's sufficiency for making judgments, and (c) revise the data-gathering plan as necessary to achieve this sufficiency.

corroboration   The extent to which enough objective evidence has been gathered to confirm that an observation is acceptable for use by an appraisal team.

coverage   The extent to which objective evidence gathered addresses both the model and organizational scope of an appraisal.

data collection session   An activity during which information is gathered that will later be used as the basis for observation formulation or corroboration. Data collection sessions (or activities) include the administration and/or analysis of instruments, document reviews, interviews, and presentations.

draft findings   Preliminary findings created by an appraisal team after consolidating and synthesizing valid observations. Draft findings are provided to appraisal participants for validation of accuracy.

equivalent staging   A target staging created using the continuous representation that is defined so that the results of using the target staging can be compared to the maturity levels of the staged representation. Such staging permits benchmarking of progress among organizations, enterprises, and projects, regardless of the CMMI representation used. The organization may implement components of CMMI models beyond those reported as part of equivalent staging. Equivalent staging is only a measure to relate how the organization is compared to other organizations in terms of maturity levels.

evaluation   (See "capability evaluation.")

findings   The conclusions of an appraisal that identify the most important issues, problems, or opportunities within the appraisal scope. Findings include, at a minimum, strengths and weaknesses based on valid observations.

instruments   Artifacts used in an appraisal for the collection and presentation of data (such as questionnaires and organizational unit information packets).

interviews   A meeting of appraisal team members with appraisal participants for the purpose of gathering information relative to work processes in place.

lead appraiser   A person who has achieved recognition from an authorizing body to perform as an appraisal team leader for a particular appraisal method.

objective evidence   Qualitative or quantitative information, records, or statements of fact pertaining to the characteristics of an item or service or to the existence and implementation of a process element, which are based on observation, measurement, or test and are verifiable.

observation   A written record that represents the appraisal team members' understanding of information either seen or heard during the appraisal data collection activities. The written record may take the form of a statement or may take alternative forms, as long as the information content is preserved.

organizational unit   The part of an organization that is the subject of an appraisal (also known as the organizational scope of the appraisal). An organizational unit deploys one or more processes that have a coherent process context and operates within a coherent set of business objectives. An organizational unit is typically part of a larger organization, although in a small organization, the organizational unit may be the whole organization.

process attribute   A measurable characteristic of process performance applicable to any process.

process attribute outcomes   The results of achievement of a process attribute.

process context   The set of factors documented in the appraisal input that influences the judgment and comparability of appraisal ratings. These include, but are not limited to, (a) the size of the organizational unit to be appraised, (b) the demographics of the organizational unit, (c) the application domain of the products or services, (d) the size, criticality, and complexity of the products or services, and (e) the quality characteristics of the products or services.

process profile   The set of goal ratings assigned to the process areas in the scope of the appraisal. In CMMI, also known as the process area profile.

rating   (See "appraisal rating.")

satisfied   Rating given to a goal when the associated generic or specific practices (or acceptable alternative practices) are judged to be implemented and the aggregate of weaknesses does not have a significant negative impact on goal achievement. Rating given to a process area when all of its goals are rated "satisfied."

strength   Exemplary or noteworthy implementation of a CMMI model practice.

tailoring   (See "appraisal tailoring.")

valid observation   An observation that the appraisal team members agree is (a) accurate, (b) corroborated, and (c) consistent with other accurate and corroborated observations.

weakness   The ineffective, or lack of, implementation of one or more CMMI model practices.

Appendix B

Practice Implementation Indicator Descriptions

This appendix[1] provides a starting point to help identify direct and indirect evidence for each practice in the model. It is critical to understand that these work products are a result of executing the processes defined by the project/organization. This list can be tailored by an organization to enable the collection of objective evidence in preparation for an appraisal. The intent of this document is not to redefine the CMMI. Be careful in using this information.

For each process area, the specific goals and practices are presented with both direct and indirect example work products. Each generic practice for capability level 2 and 3 is also presented in this appendix. Each appraisal team will determine the specific direct and indirect evidence required for an appraisal. The appraisal team may not agree with

---

[1] The authors started with the Practice Implementation Indicator Descriptions that were developed by the CMMI Project Appraisal Methods Expert Team (AMET) for this appendix. The authors created PA PIIDs that were not covered by the AMET work. Those that were used were modified based on the authors' experience. The original PIIDs can be found on the SEI Web site.

this document, or they might agree one day and disagree another. Volatility in PIIDs has been shown to be relatively high. An organization might consider creating a measure on PIIDs to track the appraisal team's expectation volatility.

The work products listed in the PIIDs are generic in nature. An organization can choose the best way to document each of them. In some cases, several work products may actually exist in a single document. The key is that the documentation system and structure of the work products are generated by the processes and meet the needs of the organization. With that in mind, the following sections list possible objective evidence for each practice.

Causal Analysis and Resolution (CAR) PA

CAR SG   Root causes of defects and other problems are systematically determined.

CAR SP 1.1   Select the defects and other problems for analysis.

> Example Direct Artifacts
>   Defect data
>   Problem data
> *Example Indirect Artifacts*
>   Minutes of defect data selection meeting
>   Analysis results of defects or problems

CAR SP 1.2-1   Perform causal analysis of selected defects and other problems and propose actions to address them.

> *Example Direct Artifacts*
>   Defect data analysis results
>   Problem analysis results
>   Corrective action proposals
> *Example Indirect Artifacts*
>   Minutes of data or problem analysis meetings
>   Status of corrective action proposals

CAR SG 2   Root causes of defects and other problems are systematically addressed to prevent their future occurrence.

CAR SP 2.1-1   Implement the selected action proposals that were developed in causal analysis.

> *Example Direct Artifacts*
>   List of corrective actions selected for implementation
>   Completed corrective action
> *Example Indirect Artifacts*
>   Minutes of selection meeting
>   Minutes of corrective action review or approval

CAR SP 2.2-1   Evaluate the effect of changes on process performance.

Example Direct Artifacts
  Measures showing effectiveness of the corrective action
Example Indirect Artifacts
  Results of the assessment of the corrected process
  Process deployment updates or other records

CAR SP 2.3-1   Record causal analysis and resolution data for use across the project and organization.

Example Direct Artifacts
  Causal analysis records or reports
Example Indirect Artifacts
  Analysis meeting minutes showing recording of the analysis
  Approval of process improvements

Configuration Management (CM) PA

CM SG 1   Baselines of identified work products are established.

CM SP 1.1-1   Identify the configuration items, components, and related work products that will be placed under configuration management.

Example Direct Artifacts
  Identified configuration items list
  Configuration management plan
  Configuration management life cycle for controlled items (such as owner, point at which placed under control, degree of control, and change approval)
Example Indirect Artifacts
  Configuration management plan CCB records
  Configuration management plan approvals
  Documented criteria for selecting configuration items

CM SP 1.2-1   Establish and maintain a configuration management and change management system for controlling work products.

Example Direct Artifacts
  CM plan, describing tools and mechanisms for storage, retrieval, multiple levels of control
  Configuration management system with controlled work products
  Change request database
  Configuration management and change management procedures
Example Indirect Artifacts
  CM library records and reports (such as baseline contents, level of controlled items, CCB status, and audit reports)
  Change management database reports
  Records of the revision of the configuration management structure, as necessary
  CM system backup and archive media

CM SP 1.3-1   Create or release baselines for internal use and for delivery to the customer.

Example Direct Artifacts
Baselines
Descriptions of baselines
Baseline identifiers with defined and controlled contents (configuration items)
Example Indirect Artifacts
Configuration management records and reports
CCB meeting minutes
Change documentation and version control associated with a baseline
Baseline generation/release procedures, scripts, transmittal documents
CM tool or repository demo (such as baselines, items, nodes, and branches)
Baseline audits

CM SG 2   Changes to the work products under configuration management are tracked and controlled.

CM SP 2.1-1   Track change requests for the configuration items.

Example Direct Artifacts
Change requests
Change request tracking products (such as change request database, reports, logs, closure status, and metrics)
Recorded evaluation and disposition of change requests (such as review, authorization, and approval of changes)
Example Indirect Artifacts
Change request impact analyses
CCB / stakeholder review records (such as logs and meeting minutes)
Configuration item revision history

CM SP 2.2-1   Control changes to the content of the configuration items.

Example Direct Artifacts
Revision history of configuration items
Revised configuration items and baselines incorporating approved changes (such as CCB approval)
Example Indirect Artifacts
Archives of the baselines
Configuration management records and reports describing the revision status of baselines and configuration items
Impact analyses, reviews, or regression tests to ensure the integrity of baseline revisions
Change request review and tracking products (such as checklists, evaluation criteria, reports, logs, closure status, and metrics)
Recorded evaluation and disposition of change requests (such as review, authorization, and approval of changes)

CM SG 3   Integrity of baselines is established and maintained.

CM SP 3.1-1   Establish and maintain records describing configuration items.

Example Direct Artifacts
  Records describing content, status, and version of configuration items and baselines.
  Reports describing configuration item status, available to affected individuals and groups (such as CM library reports and baseline access)
  Multiple versions of configuration item records, maintained over time
Example Indirect Artifacts
  Revision history of configuration items
  Change request logs or database
  Copy of the change requests
  Status of configuration items

CM SP 3.2-1   Perform configuration audits to maintain integrity of the configuration baselines.

Example Direct Artifacts
  Configuration audit results
Example Indirect Artifacts
  Action items (for discrepancies determined as a result of configuration audits)
  Criteria and checklists used to conduct configuration audits
  Quality inspection records
  Configuration audit schedules and descriptions
  Minutes of meetings in which the accuracy and contents of baselines or releases are reviewed
  Tools or reports to verify configuration baseline contents

Decision Analysis and Resolution (DAR) PA

DAR SG 1   Decisions are based on an evaluation of alternatives using established criteria.

DAR SP 1.1-1   Establish and maintain guidelines to determine which issues are subject to a formal evaluation process.

Example Direct Artifacts
  Guidelines for when to apply a formal evaluation process
Example Indirect Artifacts
  Criteria or checklists for determining when to apply a formal evaluation process
  Process description for conducting formal evaluations and selection of applicable decision-making techniques
  Identified set of typical issues subject to a formal evaluation process

DAR SP 1.2-1   Establish and maintain the criteria for evaluating alternatives and the relative ranking of these criteria.

Example Direct Artifacts
  Documented evaluation criteria
  Rankings of criteria importance

Example Indirect Artifacts
  Traceability of criteria to documented sources (such as requirements, assumptions, and business objectives)
  Guidance for determining and applying evaluation criteria (such as ranges, scales, formulas, and rationale)
  Rationale for selection and rejection of evaluation criteria

DAR SP 1.3-1   Identify alternative solutions to address issues.

Example Direct Artifacts
  Identified alternatives
Example Indirect Artifacts
  Decision report listing alternatives evaluated
  Results of brainstorming sessions, interviews, or other techniques used to identify potential solutions
  Research resources and references (such as literature surveys)

DAR SP 1.4-1   Select the evaluation methods.

Example Direct Artifacts
  Selected evaluation methods
Example Indirect Artifacts
  Decision report listing evaluation method selected
  List of candidate or preferred evaluation methods
  Guidance on selection of appropriate evaluation methods

DAR SP 1.5-1   Evaluate alternative solutions using the documented criteria.

Example Direct Artifacts
  Evaluation results
  Conclusions or findings from evaluations
Example Indirect Artifacts
  Presentation of results and minutes of the review or meeting
  Evaluated assumptions and constraints for application of evaluation criteria or interpretation of results (such as uncertainty and significance)
  Completed evaluation forms, checklists, or assigned criteria
  Results of simulations, modeling, prototypes, pilots, life-cycle cost analyses, studies, and so on, performed on potential solutions

DAR SP 1.6-1   Select solutions from the alternatives based on the evaluation criteria.

Example Direct Artifacts
  Documented results and rationale of the decision
Example Indirect Artifacts
  Approval of the final selected solution by stakeholders
  Risk assessment of solutions or execution of the decision-making process

Integrated Project Management (IPM) PA

IPM SG 1   The project is conducted using a defined process that is tailored from the organization's set of standard processes.

IPM SP 1.1-1   Establish and maintain the project's defined process.

Example Direct Artifacts
  Project's defined process
  Tailoring form
Example Indirect Artifacts
  Peer Review results of the project's defined process
  Approved waivers to deviations from the organization's standard
  process

IPM SP 1.2-1   Use the organizational process assets and measurement repository for estimating and planning the project's activities.

Example Direct Artifacts
  Project plans following templates/guidelines
  Records of independent validation of historical data
  Records of assumptions and rationale used to select the historical data
  for the project estimates
  Revision history of project estimates
Example Indirect Artifacts
  Organizational measurement database/repository
  Organizational asset library/repository
  Bases of Estimates (BOEs)
  Project's defined process that includes the size and complexity of tasks
  and work products to be produced

IPM SP 1.3-1   Integrate the project plan and the other plans that affect the
project to describe the project's defined process.

Example Direct Artifacts
  Integrated plans
  Plan changes reviewed by relevant stakeholders
Example Indirect Artifacts
  Project schedule and schedule dependencies
  Meeting minutes from stakeholder reviews of the project plan

IPM SP 1.4-1   Manage the project using the project plan, the other plans that
affect the project, and the project's defined process.

Example Direct Artifacts
  Work products created by performing the project's defined process
  Collected measures ("actuals") and progress records or reports
  Revised requirements, plans, and commitments
  Corrective actions based on discrepancies versus plan
  Records of reviews held to monitor progress against project plans and
  corrective actions taken as necessary
Example Indirect Artifacts
  Project plan and other plans that affect the project
  Project's defined process
  Criteria or checklists used to track and manage transition across the
  project or product life cycle

IPM SP 1.5-1   Contribute work products, measures, and documented experiences to the organizational process assets.

Example Direct Artifacts
Proposed improvements to the organization's process assets
Actual process and product measures collected from the project
Documentation (such as exemplary process descriptions, plans, training modules, checklists, and lessons learned)
Project best practices and lessons learned
Records of the project recording process and product measures in the organization's measurement repository

Example Indirect Artifacts
Organizational measurement database/repository that reflects actual process and product measures from the projects
Organizational asset library/repository that provides evidence that work products and lessons learned are being populated by the projects
Records of proposed process improvements and disposition

IPM SG 2   Coordination and collaboration of the project with relevant stakeholders is conducted.

IPM SP 2.1-1   Manage the involvement of the relevant stakeholders in the project.

Example Direct Artifacts
Agendas and schedules for collaborative activities
Documented issues (such as issues with the customer requirements, product and product-component requirements, product architecture, and product design)
Issues and dispositions for resolving stakeholder interfaces and misunderstanding
Records that show relevant stakeholder involvement is maintained

Example Indirect Artifacts
Milestone/stakeholder review meeting minutes
Organizational chart
Records of reviews, demonstrations, or testing on work products produced to satisfy commitments to meet the requirements of the recipient projects
Project plan, identifying relevant stakeholders
Plan for stakeholder involvement
Project schedule(s) that identify critical dependencies with relevant stakeholders

IPM SP 2.2-1   Participate with relevant stakeholders to identify, negotiate, and track critical dependencies.

Example Direct Artifacts
Defects, issues, and action items arising from reviews with relevant stakeholders
Critical dependencies
Commitments to address critical dependencies

Status of critical dependencies
Records of reviews to address critical dependencies and corrective actions taken

Example Indirect Artifacts
Stakeholder milestone/project status reviews
Project plan, identifying relevant stakeholders
Project schedule(s) that identify critical dependencies with relevant stakeholders
Updated project plans reflecting and associated artifacts demonstrating negotiating and tracking

IPM SP 2.3-1   Resolve issues with relevant stakeholders.

Example Direct Artifacts
Relevant stakeholder-coordination issues
Status of relevant stakeholder coordination issues
Records of tracking issues to closure with relevant stakeholder involvement

Example Indirect Artifacts
Reviews, reports, or briefings communicating issues to stakeholders
Issue tracking database with evidence of issues status being tracked and issues being resolved
Evidence of escalation of issues to managers as needed

IPM SC 3   The project is conducted using the project's shared vision.

IPM SP 3.1-1   Identify expectations, constraints, interfaces, and operational conditions applicable to the project's shared vision.

Example Direct Artifacts
Organizational expectations
Stakeholder constraints
Operational conditions
External interfaces

Example Indirect Artifacts
Minutes of customer reviews
Stakeholder review minutes

IPM SP 3.2-1   Establish and maintain a shared vision for the project.

Example Direct Artifacts
Shared vision
Example Indirect Artifacts
Shared vision review minutes
Shared vision approval

IPM SG 4   The integrated teams needed to execute the project are identified, defined, structured, and tasked.

IPM SP 4.1-1   Determine the integrated team structure that will best meet the project objectives and constraints.

Example Direct Artifacts
   Integrated Team Structure (Organizational Chart)
Example Indirect Artifacts
   Minutes of team structure stakeholder review

IPM SP 4.2-1   Develop a preliminary distribution of requirements, responsibilities, authorities, tasks, and interfaces to teams in the selected integrated team structure.

Example Direct Artifacts
   Preliminary Project Team Organization Plan
      Team requirements assignments
      Team responsibilities assignments
      Team authorities assignments
      Team tasks assignments
      Team interface assignments
Example Indirect Artifacts
   Preliminary Project Team Organization Plan Review minutes
   Preliminary Project Team Organization Plan Review approval

IPM SP 4.3-1   Establish and maintain teams in the integrated team structure.

Example Direct Artifacts
   Project Team Organization Plan
   Project Team Structure chart
Example Indirect Artifacts
   Project Team Organization Plan Review minutes
   Project Team Organization Plan Review approval

Integrated Supplier Management (ISM) PA

ISM SG 1   Potential sources of products that best fit the needs of the project are identified, analyzed, and selected.

ISM SP 1.1-1   Identify and analyze potential sources of products that may be used to satisfy the project's requirements.

Example Direct Artifacts
   Potential supplier list
   Supplier information
   Supplier sourcing trade study results
Example Indirect Artifacts
   Supplier information database
   Minutes of supplier analysis meeting

ISM SP 1.2-1   Use a formal evaluation process to determine which sources of custom-made and off-the-shelf products to use.

Example Direct Artifacts
   Sourcing trade study results
Example Indirect Artifacts
   Minutes of trade study review meeting

ISM SG 2   Work is coordinated with suppliers to ensure the supplier agreement is executed appropriately.

ISM SP 2.1-1   Monitor and analyze selected processes used by the supplier.

Example Direct Artifacts
  Supplier activity reports
  Supplier performance reports
  Supplier analysis meeting minutes
Example Indirect Artifacts
  Technical interchange meeting minutes
  List of selected processes to be monitored

ISM SP 2.2-1   For custom-made products, evaluate selected supplier work products.

Example Direct Artifacts
  Supplier work product review material
  List of supplier work products selected
Example Indirect Artifacts
  Supplier work product review minutes
  Technical interchange meeting minutes

ISM SP 2.3-1   Revise the supplier agreement or relationship, as appropriate, to reflect changes in conditions.

Example Direct Artifacts
  Revisions to supplier agreement
  Change requests for supplier agreement
Example Indirect Artifacts
  CCB meeting minutes showing supplier agreement actions
  Supplier agreement review minutes

Integrated Teaming (IT) PA

IT SG 1   A team composition that provides the knowledge and skills required to deliver the team's product is established and maintained.

IT SP 1.1-1   Identify and define the team's specific internal tasks to generate the team's expected output.

Example Direct Artifacts
  Team deliverables
  Task descriptors
Example Indirect Artifacts
  Team task review minutes
  Team status reports

IT SP 1.2-1   Identify the knowledge, skills, and functional expertise needed to perform team tasks.

Example Direct Artifacts
  List of disciplines needed for team
  Skills list for team
  Team training model

Example Indirect Artifacts
    Team profile of skills and disciplines
    Training records for team members

IT SP 1.3-1   Assign the appropriate personnel to be team members based on required knowledge and skills.

Example Direct Artifacts
    List of team members by discipline
    Team structure chart
    Budget for team
Example Indirect Artifacts
    Team member assignment approval
    Requisition for team members
    Time records for team members

IT SG 2   Operation of the integrated team is governed according to established principles.

IT SP 2.1-1   Establish and maintain a shared vision for the integrated team that is aligned with any overarching or higher level vision.

Example Direct Artifacts
    Documented shared vision
    Meeting materials for team kickoff
Example Indirect Artifacts
    Meeting minutes for team kickoff

IT SP 2.2-1   Establish and maintain a team charter based on the integrated team's shared vision and overall team objectives.

Example Direct Artifacts
    Team charter
Example Indirect Artifacts
    Approval of team charter by team members and key stakeholders

IT SP 2.3-1   Clearly define and maintain each team member's roles and responsibilities.

Example Direct Artifacts
    Team charter showing roles and responsibilities of team members
Example Indirect Artifacts
    Approval of team charter by team members and key stakeholders

IT SP 2.4-1   Establish and maintain integrated team operating procedures.

Example Direct Artifacts
    Tailored procedures
Example Indirect Artifacts
    Approval of tailored team procedures

IT SP 2.5-1   Establish and maintain collaboration among interfacing teams.

Example Direct Artifacts
    Team inputs to IMP/IMS
    Team meeting minutes

Example Indirect Artifacts
> Reports showing team collaboration
> Team interface work products

Measurement and Analysis (MA) PA

MA SG 1   Measurement objectives and activities are aligned with identified information needs and objectives.

MA SP 1.1-1   Establish and maintain measurement objectives that are derived from identified information needs and objectives.

Example Direct Artifacts
> Information needs and objectives
> Measurement objectives

Example Indirect Artifacts
> Alignment between business goals, measurement objectives/goals, information needs/objectives
> Reviews of measurement objectives with affected stakeholders (such as management, providers, and users)

MA SP 1.2-1   Specify measures to address the measurement objectives.

Example Direct Artifacts
> Specifications of base and derived measures
> Operational definitions for base and derived measures

Example Indirect Artifacts
> Linkage between measures and project/organization measurement objectives and information needs
> Review of specifications with stakeholders
> List of prioritized measures

MA SP 1.3-1   Specify how measurement data will be obtained and stored.

Example Direct Artifacts
> Data collection and storage procedures
> Data collection descriptions, including who (responsibilities), how (procedures and tools), when (frequency), where (repository)

Example Indirect Artifacts
> Data collection mechanisms and supporting tools (automatic or manual)
> Raw data collected, time tagged, and stored
> Measurement repository

MA SP 1.4-1   Specify how measurement data will be analyzed and reported.

Example Direct Artifacts
> Analysis specification and procedures
> Analysis descriptions, including who (responsibilities), how (procedures and tools), when (frequency), where (repository), and how the results will be used

Example Indirect Artifacts
> Data analysis tools
> Results of data analyses (such as graphs and reports)

Alignment of data analyses with measurement objectives (such as traceability to information needs and decision making)
Minutes of measurement analyses review
Criteria for evaluating the utility of measurement and analysis data

MA SG 2   Measurement results that address identified information needs and objectives are provided.

MA SP 2.1-1   Obtain specified measurement data.

Example Direct Artifacts
Base and derived measurement data
Raw data collected, time tagged, and stored in accordance with defined data collection procedures
Derived measures calculated from collected base measures
Example Indirect Artifacts
Measurement repository populated with the specified measures
Results of data integrity tests
Results of integrity checks (such as tools, forms, and reviews); reports of invalid or discarded data

MA SP 2.2-1   Analyze and interpret measurement data.

Example Direct Artifacts
Analysis results (such as graphs and reports) and conclusions (preliminary or final)
Example Indirect Artifacts
Representations for analysis results (such as tables, charts, and histograms)
Minutes of measurement analyses meetings (briefings, minutes, action items, and so on)
Follow-up analysis performed to address areas of concern

MA SP 2.3-1   Manage and store measurement data, measurement specifications, and analysis results.

Example Direct Artifacts
Stored data inventory
Measurement repository with historical data and results
Senior management review materials showing measures
Example Indirect Artifacts
Senior management review meeting minutes
Measurement repository, with access restriction to the stored data

MA SP 2.4-1   Report results of measurement and analysis activities to all relevant stakeholders.

Example Direct Artifacts
Senior management reviews materials showing measures
Delivered reports and related analysis results
Example Indirect Artifacts
Senior management reviews meeting minutes
Presentations of data analyses and reports

Organizational Environment for Integration (OEI) PA

OEI SG 1   An infrastructure that maximizes the productivity of people, and the collaboration necessary for integration is provided.

OEI SP 1.1-1   Establish and maintain a shared vision for the organization.

Example Direct Artifacts
　　Organization shared vision
Example Indirect Artifacts
　　Communication materials for shared vision

OEI SP 1.2-1   Establish and maintain an integrated work environment that supports IPPD by enabling collaboration and concurrent development.

Example Direct Artifacts
　　Requirements for integrated work environment
　　Integrated work environment structure chart
Example Indirect Artifacts
　　Demonstrations of components of the integrated work environment
　　Trade studies for selecting components of the integrated work environment

OEI SP 1.3-1   Identify the unique skills needed to support the IPPD environment.

Example Direct Artifacts
　　IPPD organization training model
　　Training plan
Example Indirect Artifacts
　　Individual training records
　　IPPD training class records

OEI SG 2   People are managed to nurture the integrative and collaborative behaviors of an IPPD environment.

OEI SP 2.1-1   Establish and maintain leadership mechanisms to enable timely collaboration.

Example Direct Artifacts
　　Organizational process for issue resolution
　　Leadership training model
Example Indirect Artifacts
　　Approval of organizational process
　　Leadership training records

OEI SP 2.2-1   Establish and maintain incentives for adopting and demonstrating integrative and collaborative behaviors at all levels of the organization.

Example Direct Artifacts
　　Incentive plan
Example Indirect Artifacts
　　Records showing incentives awarded across the organization

OEI SP 2.3-1   Establish and maintain organizational guidelines to balance team and home organization responsibilities.

Example Direct Artifacts
  Organizational guidelines for team/functional organization
  responsibilities
Example Indirect Artifacts
  Project use of organizational guidelines
  Team use of organizational guidelines

Organizational Innovation and Deployment (OID) PA

OID SG 1   Process and technology improvements that contribute to meeting
quality and process-performance objectives are selected.

OID SP 1.1-1   Collect and analyze process- and technology-improvement
proposals.

Example Direct Artifacts
  Improvement proposals' analysis results
Example Indirect Artifacts
  Change requests resulting from proposed improvements
  Action items for proposed improvements

OID SP 1.2-1   Identify and analyze innovative improvements that could
increase the organization's quality and process performance.

Example Direct Artifacts
  Candidate innovative improvement proposals
  Candidate innovative improvement proposal analyses
Example Indirect Artifacts
  Change requests resulting from proposed improvements
  Action items for proposed improvements

OID SP 1.3-1   Pilot process and technology improvements to select which
ones to implement.

Example Direct Artifacts
  Pilot activity report
Example Indirect Artifacts
  Lessons learned report
  Review minutes for improvement pilots

OID SP 1.4-1   Select process- and technology-improvement proposals for
deployment across the organization.

Example Direct Artifacts
  Analysis report showing selection of process improvements
  Change requests for process improvements
Example Indirect Artifacts
  Analysis of meeting minutes
  Deployment work products for process improvements

OID SG 2   Measurable improvements to the organization's processes and
technologies are continually and systematically deployed.

OID SP 2.1-1   Establish and maintain the plans for deploying the selected process and technology improvements.

Example Direct Artifacts
  Deployment plan
Example Indirect Artifacts
  Review minutes of deployment plan

OID SP 2.2-1   Manage the deployment of the selected process and technology improvements.

Example Direct Artifacts
  Updated training materials
  Results of deployment activities
  Deployment scorecard
Example Indirect Artifacts
  Labor charges for deployment activities
  Presentation of training records
  Minutes of senior management review of deployment scorecard

OID SP 2.3-1   Measure the effects of the deployed process and technology improvements.

Example Direct Artifacts
  Measurement data in repository
  Analysis of measurement data
Example Indirect Artifacts
  Measurement analysis meeting minutes

Organizational Process Definition (OPD) PA

OPD SG 1   A set of organizational process assets is established and maintained.

OPD SP 1.1-1   Establish and maintain the organization's set of standard processes.

Example Direct Artifacts
  Organization's set of standard processes
  Process architectures describing relationships among process elements
  Revisions to the organization's set of standard processes (such as revised processes, reviews, and so on)
Example Indirect Artifacts
  Process and product standards
  Process for development, review, and revision of organizational standard processes and assets
  Results of peer reviews of the organization's set of standard processes

OPD SP 1.2-1   Establish and maintain descriptions of the life-cycle process models approved for use in the organization.

Example Direct Artifacts
  Descriptions of life-cycle models
  Revisions to the organization's set of life-cycle process models (such as revised models, reviews, and so on)

Example Indirect Artifacts
> Guidance and criteria on selection of life-cycle models based on the needs and characteristics of the project and the organization's needs
> Approval records of the life-cycle model descriptions

OPD SP 1.3-1   Establish and maintain the tailoring criteria and guidelines for the organization's set of standard processes.

Example Direct Artifacts
> Tailoring guidelines for the organization's set of standard processes
> Revisions to the organization's tailoring criteria and guidelines (such as revised guidelines, reviews, and so on)

Example Indirect Artifacts
> Documented results of tailoring guideline peer reviews
> Process compliance review checklists

OPD SP 1.4-1   Establish and maintain the organization's measurement repository.

Example Direct Artifacts
> Definition of the common set of product and process measures for the organization's set of standard processes
> Organization's measurement repository (such as the repository structure and support environment)
> Revisions to the organization's measurement repository (such as revised measures, collected measures, reviews, and so on)

Example Indirect Artifacts
> Organization's measurement data
> Analysis/rationale supporting definition of measures related to products and organization standard process (elements)
> Procedures for collection, storage, analysis of organizational measures
> Logs or records indicating population and use of measurement repository
> Records of communication describing the measurement repository, its use, and population

OPD SP 1.5-1   Establish and maintain the organization's library of process-related assets.

Example Direct Artifacts
> Organization's process asset library
> Revisions to the organization's library of process-related assets (such as revised library and assets, reviews, and so on)

Example Indirect Artifacts
> Catalog of items in the organization's process asset library
> Selected items to be included in the organization's process asset library
> Collection of best practices
> Criteria and procedures for adding items to library
> Reviews of process asset library contents

Organizational Process Focus (OPF) PA

OPF SG 1   Strengths, weaknesses, and improvement opportunities for the organization's processes are identified periodically and as needed.

OPF SP 1.1-1   Establish and maintain the description of the process needs and objectives for the organization.

Example Direct Artifacts
   Organization's process needs and objectives
   Revisions to the organization's process and business objectives/goals (such as revised business objectives, evidence of reviews, and so on)
Example Indirect Artifacts
   Review and approval of process needs and objectives
   Process and product policies, standards, and guidelines (notation, level of detail, and so on)
   Characterization of current organization processes (processes currently in use, process and product standards enforced at either the enterprise or company level, or imposed by the customers of the organization)

OPF SP 1.2-1   Appraise the processes of the organization periodically and as needed to maintain an understanding of their strengths and weaknesses.

Example Direct Artifacts
   Plans for the organization's process appraisals
   Appraisal findings that address strengths and weaknesses of the organization's processes
      Final finding presentations
      Final finding appraisal reports
      Data in other formats such as a process improvement tracking tool

Example Indirect Artifacts
   Improvement recommendations for the organization's processes
   Appraisal records or reports (plan, scope, participants, interview schedules, list of artifacts examined, and so on)
   Action plans to address appraisal findings
   Process improvement progress records (such as metrics, trends, and analyses)
   Appraisal briefings describing the method to be used, purpose, and so on

OPF SP 1.3-1   Identify improvements to the organization's processes and process assets.

Example Direct Artifacts
   Identification of improvements for the organization's processes
   Prioritized list of planned process improvements
Example Indirect Artifacts
   Analysis of candidate process improvements
   Measurements and analysis of processes
   Reports of process performance

Reviews of lessons learned

Meeting minutes from process improvement–related reviews and planning sessions

Documented criteria for prioritization of improvement opportunities

OPF SG 2 Improvements are planned and implemented, organizational process assets are deployed, and process-related experiences are incorporated into the organizational process assets.

OPF SP 2.1-1 Establish and maintain process action plans to address improvements to the organization's processes and process assets.

Example Direct Artifacts

Organization's approved process action plans

Review and revision of the organization's approved process action plans (such as revised objectives, reviews, and so on)

Example Indirect Artifacts

Review and approval of the action plans by senior management and the management steering committee

Results of stakeholder reviews of process action plans

Documented infrastructure for process improvement with clearly defined roles and responsibilities (such as management, process owners, process group, action teams, and practitioners)

OPF SP 2.2-1 Implement process action plans across the organization.

Example Direct Artifacts

Status and results of implementing process action plans

Example Indirect Artifacts

Process improvement status reviews and briefings (management reviews and technical reviews)

Records of effort and expenditure associated with implementation (such as metrics, analyses, and progress reports)

Commitments among the various process action teams

Negotiated commitments and revisions to process action plans

Issues identified from implementation of process action plans

Records indicating identification, tracking, and resolution of issues related to implementation of process action plans

OPF SP 2.3-1 Deploy organizational process assets across the organization.

Example Direct Artifacts

Status of deploying the organizational process assets

Documentation of changes to the organizational process assets

Process asset library (PAL)

Generated organizational process assets, methods, and tools

Example Indirect Artifacts

Records of effort and expenditure associated with deployment

Training materials for deploying the organizational process assets and changes to organizational process assets

Support materials for deploying the organizational process assets and changes to organizational process assets

Deployment issue identification and resolution records
Records of training or orientation provided on the new process assets and population and use of PAL (if applicable)

OPF SP 2.4-1   Incorporate process-related work products, measures, and improvement information derived from planning and performing the process into the organization's process assets.

Example Direct Artifacts
Records of the organization's process-improvement activities
Revisions to organization's process assets
Process-improvement proposals
Measurements on the organizational process assets
Process lessons learned
Example Indirect Artifacts
Reviews including process evaluations, process proposals, tracking of improvement efforts, and so on
Improvement recommendations for the organizational process assets
Information on the organizational process assets and improvements to them
Analysis of process performance measures and process assets
Lessons learned repository
Collection of best practices

Organizational Process Performance (OPP) PA

OPP SG 1   Baselines and models that characterize the expected process performance of the organization's set of standard processes are established and maintained.

OPP SP 1.1-1   Select the processes or process elements in the organization's set of standard processes that are to be included in the organization's process performance analyses.

Example Direct Artifacts
Selected processes or process elements
Example Indirect Artifacts
Review of process selection results

OPP SP 1.2-1   Establish and maintain definitions of the measures that are to be included in the organization's process performance analyses.

Example Direct Artifacts
Measure definitions
Example Indirect Artifacts
Minutes of measure definitions review
Release of measurement specifications

OPP SP 1.3-1   Establish and maintain quantitative objectives for quality and process performance for the organization.

Example Direct Artifacts
  Organization's quality and process–performance objectives
Example Indirect Artifacts
  Minutes of objective review

OPP SP 1.4-1   Establish and maintain the organization's process performance baselines.

Example Direct Artifacts
  Process performance baseline
Example Indirect Artifacts
  Measurement repository
  Process performance baseline communications

OPP SP 1.5-1   Establish and maintain the process performance models for the organization's set of standard processes.

Example Direct Artifacts
  Process performance models
Example Indirect Artifacts
  Minutes of process performance model reviews

Organizational Training (OT) PA

OT SG 1   A training capability that supports the organization's management and technical roles is established and maintained.

OT SP 1.1-1   Establish and maintain the strategic training needs of the organization.

Example Direct Artifacts
  Training needs
Example Indirect Artifacts
  Review and revision history of the strategic training needs of the organization
  Identification of roles and skills needed
  List of required training courses needed

OT SP 1.2-1   Determine which training needs are the responsibility of the organization and which will be left to the individual project or support group.

Example Direct Artifacts
  A list of the training to be provided by the organization
Example Indirect Artifacts
  Organization training records
  Common project and support group training needs
  Lists of special training needs required by projects or support groups

OT SP 1.3-1   Establish and maintain an organizational training tactical plan.

Example Direct Artifacts
  Organizational training tactical plan
  Adjustments or revision history of the organizational training tactical plan

Example Indirect Artifacts
  Lists of training courses, prerequisites, skills, schedules, funding, roles, and responsibilities
  Reviews or status reports tracking implementation progress (such as schedule and remaining budget) of the organizational training tactical plan

OT SP 1.4-1   Establish and maintain training capability to address organizational training needs.

Example Direct Artifacts
  Training materials and supporting artifacts
  Analysis and revisions of training materials and resources
  Instructor certifications
Example Indirect Artifacts
  Organization's training curriculum and course descriptions
  Analysis of whether to acquire training or provide in-house
  criteria for instructor qualifications
  Periodic reviews of training capability and resources

OT SG 2   Training necessary for individuals to perform their roles effectively is provided.

OT SP 2.1-1   Deliver the training following an organizational training plan.

Example Direct Artifacts
  Delivered training course
  Training records (schedule, instructor, and attendance)
Example Indirect Artifacts
  Training delivery reports or metrics (such as planned versus actual)
  Training curriculum, based on assigned role
  Prioritized list of pending training attendees

OT SP 2.2-1   Establish and maintain records of the organizational training.

Example Direct Artifacts
  Training records
  Attendance records and approved waivers
Example Indirect Artifacts
  Skills matrix
  Training repository
  Training metrics or reports

OT SP 2.3-1   Assess the effectiveness of the organization's training program.

Example Direct Artifacts
  Training program performance assessments
  Reviews, analyses, or reports of organizational training effectiveness and alignment with organization objectives
Example Indirect Artifacts
  Training effectiveness surveys
  Instructor evaluation forms
  Training examinations

Student evaluation feedback forms (of how well training met their
needs)
Metrics or analyses summarizing consolidated training results
Revised course materials, methods, or curriculum as a result of training
feedback

Product Integration (PI) PA

PI SG 1   Preparation for product integration is conducted.

PI SP 1.1-1   Determine the product-component integration sequence.

Example Direct Artifacts
Product integration sequence
Product integration plan
Example Indirect Artifacts
Meetings or presentations at which the plans for product integration are
reviewed
Rationale for selecting or rejecting integration sequences
List of components to be integrated
Integration schedules and dependencies

PI SP 1.2-2   Establish and maintain the environment needed to support the
integration of the product components.

Example Direct Artifacts
Verified environment for product integration
Product integration test bed (such as test equipment, simulators, HW
equipment, and recording devices)
Product integration plan
Descriptions or configuration of the verified environment for product
integration, revised and maintained throughout the project
Example Indirect Artifacts
Reviews of product integration environment
Support documentation for the product integration environment

PI SP 1.3.-3   Establish and maintain procedures and criteria for integration of
the product components.

Example Direct Artifacts
Product integration procedures
Product integration criteria
Revision history of integration procedures and criteria, maintained
throughout the project
Example Indirect Artifacts
Product integration inputs, outputs, expected results, and progress
criteria
Reviews or presentations of integration plans, procedures, and criteria
Test readiness reviews
Incremental build/integration plan and procedures
Criteria and checklists for product-component readiness, integration,
and evaluation

Criteria and checklists for validation, and delivery of the integrated
product

PI SG 2   The product-component interfaces, both internal and external, are
compatible.

PI SP 2.1-1   Review interface descriptions for coverage and completeness.

Example Direct Artifacts
  Minutes of interface description reviews
Example Indirect Artifacts
  Interface specifications, *interface control documents* (ICDs), *interface design
  documents* (IDDs)
  Categories of interfaces (such as environmental, physical, functional,
  and mechanical)
  List of interfaces per category
  Criteria and checklists for interface reviews

PI SP 2.2-1   Manage internal and external interface definitions, designs, and
changes for products and product components.

Example Direct Artifacts
  Interface descriptions and relationships among product components
  Interface specifications, *interface control documents* (ICDs), *interface design
  documents* (IDDs)
  List of agreed-to interfaces defined for each pair of product components,
  when applicable
  Updated interface description or agreement
Example Indirect Artifacts
  Reports from the interface control working group meetings
  Result of interface reviews (such as peer reviews, quality assurance
  inspections, design reviews, interface control working groups, CCBs,
  and action items to resolve interface issues)
  Action items for updating interfaces
  Repository of interface data (such as interface database)
  Change requests for revision to interfaces

PI SG 3   Verified product components are assembled and the integrated, verified, and validated product is delivered.

PI SP 3.1-1   Confirm, prior to assembly, that each product component
required to assemble the product has been properly identified, functions
according to its description, and that the product component interfaces comply with the interface descriptions.

Example Direct Artifacts
  Acceptance documents for received product components
  Verified acceptance test results or inspection report for product
  components
  Discrepancies identified in received product components
Example Indirect Artifacts
  Delivery receipts

Checked packing lists
Exception reports
Waivers
Configuration status reports for product components
Product integration plans and procedures
Criteria and checklists for product component readiness, delivery, integration, and evaluation

PI SP 3.2-1   Assemble product components according to the product integration sequence and available procedures.

Example Direct Artifacts
Assembled product or product components
Example Indirect Artifacts
Records indicating performance of the product integration sequence and procedures (such as integration reports, completed checklists, and configuration audits)
Recorded configuration and assembly information (such as identification, configuration status, and calibration data)
Integration status and schedule reports (such as planned versus actual components integrated)
Revisions to the integration plans or procedures

PI SP 3.3-1   Evaluate assembled product components for interface compatibility.

Example Direct Artifacts
Evaluation results (such as adaptations, configuration, and deviations)
Product integration summary reports
Exception reports
Interface evaluation reports
Milestones for completion of integration activities
Example Indirect Artifacts
Discrepancies detected during checkout of product components
Logbook of product component issues or parameters.
Regression testing results

PI SP 3.4-1   Package the assembled product or product component and deliver it to the appropriate customer.

Example Direct Artifacts
Packaged product or product components
Delivery documentation
Example Indirect Artifacts
Minutes of ship readiness review
Packing list
Certification for readiness of the operation site
Site installation surveys

Project Monitoring and Control (PMC) PA

PMC SG 1   Actual performance and progress of the project are monitored against the project plan.

PMC SP 1.1-1   Monitor the actual values of the project planning parameters against the project plan.

Example Direct Artifacts
Records of project performance
Records of significant deviations against plan
Performance actual values versus plan (such as schedule, cost, effort, work product attributes, resources, knowledge, and skills)
Comparisons of actual project performance results to estimates (for re-planning)

Example Indirect Artifacts
Earned value management metrics
Variance reports
Status reports
Relevant project management/milestone progress review materials
Identified major milestones
Project or organizational repository for performance measurements
Indications that knowledge and skills of project personnel are monitored

PMC SP 1.2-1   Monitor commitments against those identified in the project plan.

Example Direct Artifacts
Records of commitment reviews
Status reports or tracking minutes
PPQA audit reports of performance against cost, schedule, and technical commitments documented in approved plans
Reports against cost account and earned value plans
Project review records, project meeting minutes, and project presentation packages showing planned activities are performed per commitments made

Example Indirect Artifacts
Project plans, and commitments tracking system
Reviews of documented commitments and revisions as necessary (such as presentations)

PMC SP 1.3-1   Monitor risks against those identified in the project plan.

Example Direct Artifacts
Records of project risk monitoring
Periodic review and revision of risk status (such as probability, priority, and severity)

Example Indirect Artifacts
Communications of risk status to relevant stakeholders

PMC SP 1.4-1   Monitor the management of project data against the project plan.

Example Direct Artifacts
Records of data management
Data management reports (such as inventory, delivery schedules, and status)

Example Indirect Artifacts
> Results of data management reviews
> Reviews/inventories/master lists or audits of project data repository status

PMC SP 1.5-1   Monitor stakeholder involvement against the project plan.

Example Direct Artifacts
> Records of stakeholder involvement
> Project team stakeholder review presentation materials
> Stakeholder issues and status

Example Indirect Artifacts
> Project team stakeholder review minutes, action items, and action item status
> Stakeholder correspondence with issues indicated

PMC SP 1.6-1   Periodically review the project's progress, performance, and issues.

Example Direct Artifacts
> Documented project review results
> Project review packages
> Reviews of project monitoring measurements and analysis

Example Indirect Artifacts
> Project review minutes and action items
> Collection and analyses of project performance measures (schedules, effort, and deviations from plan)
> Records of communications of project status to relevant stakeholders
> Records of issues, change requests, problem reports for work products and processes

PMC SP 1.7-1   Review the accomplishments and results of the project at selected project milestones.

Example Direct Artifacts
> Milestone review packages
> Documented milestone review results

Example Indirect Artifacts
> Milestone review minutes and action items
> Documented issues from the reviews
> Milestone progress performance indicators

PMC SG 2   Corrective actions are managed to closure when the project's performance or results deviate significantly from the plan.

PMC SP 2.1-1   Collect and analyze the issues and determine the corrective actions necessary to address the issues.

Example Direct Artifacts
> List of issues needing corrective actions
> Documented analysis of issues needing corrective action

Example Indirect Artifacts
> Minutes of analysis review meeting

PMC SP 2.2-1   Take corrective action on identified issues.

Example Direct Artifacts
   Corrective action plan
Example Indirect Artifacts
   Corrective action plan status reports

PMC SP 2.3-1   Manage corrective actions to closure.

Example Direct Artifacts
   Corrective action results
   Evidence that resources have been applied and schedules have been
   followed to take the planned corrective actions on identified issues
   Corrective action status, tracking reports, or metrics (such as quantity
   open/closed and trending)
Example Indirect Artifacts
   Review and meeting minutes associated with corrective actions
   Corrective action effectiveness analysis
   Closed corrective action requests
   Revision to project plans and work products (SOW, estimates,
   requirements, commitments, resources, processes, and risks)
   incorporating the corrective actions

Project Planning (PP) PA

PP SG 1   Estimates of project planning parameters are established and
maintained.

PP SP 1.1-1   Establish a top-level *work breakdown structure* (WBS) to estimate
the scope of the project.

Example Direct Artifacts
   WBS
   Top-level WBS revision history
Example Indirect Artifacts
   Estimate based on WBS
   Task descriptions
   Work product descriptions

PP SP 1.2-1   Establish and maintain estimates of the attributes of the work
products and tasks.

Example Direct Artifacts
   Estimates of the attributes of the work products and tasks (such as size)
   Estimates, as appropriate, of labor, machinery, materials, and methods
   that will be required by the project
   Estimates revision history
Example Indirect Artifacts
   Review of estimate review meeting minutes
   Estimating tools, algorithms, and procedures showing estimated
   attributes
   Bases of Estimates (BOEs)

Use of validated models
Use of models that are calibrated with historical data

PP SP 1.3-1   Define the project life-cycle phases upon which to scope the planning effort.

Example Direct Artifacts
Project life-cycle phases
Relationships, interdependencies, and sequencing of project phases
Example Indirect Artifacts
Product life-cycle phases
List of major milestones, events, or decision gates
Risks and factors influencing life-cycle selection (such as resources, schedules, and deliverables)

PP SP 1.4-1   Estimate the project effort and cost for the work products and tasks based on estimation rationale.

Example Direct Artifacts
Project effort estimates
Project cost estimates
Documented assumptions, constraints, and rationale affecting project estimates, and identify risks
BOEs
Example Indirect Artifacts
Cost review minutes
Estimation rationale
Historical data or repository from previously executed projects
Estimating methods (such as Delphi), models, tools, algorithms, and procedures

PP SG 2   A project plan is established and maintained as the basis for managing the project.

PP SP 2.1-1   Establish and maintain the project's budget and schedule.

Example Direct Artifacts
Project plan
   Project schedules
   Schedule dependencies
   Project budget
Example Indirect Artifacts
   Project plan review minutes
   Project plan approval

PP SP 2.2-1   Identify and analyze project risks.

Example Direct Artifacts
Identified risks
Risk analysis results
Example Indirect Artifacts
Records of stakeholder involvement in risk identification activities
Criteria to be used to identify and analyze project risks

PP SP 2.3-1   Plan for the management of project data.

Example Direct Artifacts
  Data management plan
  Master list of managed data
Example Indirect Artifacts
  Project data management repository and access mechanisms
  Project data identified, collected, and distributed

PP SP 2.4-1   Plan for necessary resources to perform the project.

Example Direct Artifacts
  WBS work packages
  Staffing plans and profiles
  Critical facilities/equipment list
Example Indirect Artifacts
  Budget reviews
  Program administration requirements list
  Long lead-time items identified early

PP SP 2.5-1   Plan for needed knowledge and skills to perform the project.

Example Direct Artifacts
  Inventory of skill needs
  Staffing and new hire plans
  Plans for providing needed knowledge and skills (such as training plan)
Example Indirect Artifacts
  Databases (such as skills and training)

PP SP 2.6-1   Plan the involvement of identified stakeholders.

Example Direct Artifacts
  Stakeholder involvement plan
Example Indirect Artifacts
  Minutes of stakeholder meetings
  Stakeholder communication packages

PP SP 2.7-1   Establish and maintain the overall project plan content.

Example Direct Artifacts
  Project plan
Example Indirect Artifacts
  Approval of project plan
  Review results of project plan

PP SG 3 Commitments to the project plan are established and maintained.

PP SP 3.1-1   Review all plans that affect the project to understand project commitments.

Example Direct Artifacts
  Record of the reviews of plans that affect the project
  Review and signature cycle of the set of plans describing project scope, objectives, roles, and relationships

Example Indirect Artifacts
    Minutes of project plan coordination meetings

PP SP 3.2-1   Reconcile the project plan to reflect available and estimated resources.

Example Direct Artifacts
    Renegotiated budgets
    Revised schedules
    Revised requirements list
    Renegotiated stakeholder agreements
Example Indirect Artifacts
    Revised methods and corresponding estimating parameters (such as better tools and use of off-the-shelf components)
    Project change requests
    Project plan revision history

PP SP 3.3-1   Obtain commitment from relevant stakeholders responsible for performing and supporting plan execution.

Example Direct Artifacts
    Documented commitment by those implementing the plan
    Documented commitments by those responsible for providing resources
Example Indirect Artifacts
    Commitment review meeting minutes
    Documented requests for commitments
    Identified commitments on interfaces between elements in the project, with other projects, and organizational units

Process and Product Quality Assurance (PPQA) PA

PPQA SG 1   Adherence of the performed process and associated work products and services to applicable process descriptions, standards, and procedures is objectively evaluated.

PPQA SP 1.1-1   Objectively evaluate the designated performed processes against the applicable process descriptions, standards, and procedures.

Example Direct Artifacts
    Evaluation reports
    Noncompliance reports
Example Indirect Artifacts
    Corrective actions
    Action items for noncompliance issues, tracked to closure
    Criteria and checklists used for process and work product evaluations (such as what, when, how, and who)
    Schedule for performing process evaluations (planned, actual) at selected milestones throughout the product development life cycle
    Organizational chart or description identifying responsibility, objectivity, and reporting chain of the QA function
    Quality assurance records, reports, or database
    Records of reviews or events indicating QA involvement (such as attendance lists and signature)

PPQA SP 1.2-1   Objectively evaluate the designated work products and services against the applicable process descriptions, standards, and procedures

Example Direct Artifacts
    Evaluation reports
    Noncompliance reports
Example Indirect Artifacts
    Corrective actions
    Action items for noncompliance issues, tracked to closure
    Criteria and checklists used for work product evaluations (such as what, when, how, and who); may include sampling criteria
    Schedule for performing work product evaluations (planned, actual) at selected milestones throughout the product development life cycle
    Organizational chart or description identifying responsibility, objectivity, and reporting chain of the QA function
    Quality assurance records, reports, or database
    Records of reviews or events indicating QA involvement (such as attendance lists and signature)

PPQA SG 2   Noncompliance issues are objectively tracked and communicated, and resolution is ensured.

PPQA SP 2.1-1   Communicate quality issues and ensure resolution of noncompliance issues with the staff and managers.

Example Direct Artifacts
    Corrective action reports
    Evaluation reports
Example Indirect Artifacts
    Action items for noncompliance issues, tracked to closure
    Revised work products, standards and procedures, or waivers issued to resolve noncompliance issues
    Quality metrics and trend analyses
    Quality trends
    Reports or briefings communicating noncompliance issues to relevant stakeholders
    Evidence of reviews held periodically to receive and act upon noncompliance issues
    Tracking system or database for noncompliance issues

PPQA SP 2.2-1   Establish and maintain records of the quality assurance activities.

Example Direct Artifacts
    Evaluation logs
    Quality assurance reports
Example Indirect Artifacts
    Status reports of corrective actions
    Status reports of quality assurance activities
    Reports of quality trends
    Noncompliance actions, reports, logs, or database
    Completed evaluation checklists

Records of reviews or events indicating QA involvement (e.g.
attendance lists, signature)
Metrics or analyses used for quality assurance of processes and work
products

Quantitative Project Management (QPM) PA

QPM SG 1   The project is quantitatively managed using quality and process–
performance objectives.

QPM SP 1.1-1   Establish and maintain the project's quality and process-performance objectives.

Example Direct Artifacts
Project quality and process-performance objectives
Example Indirect Artifacts
Review of objectives

QPM SP 1.2-1   Select the subprocesses that compose the project's defined
process based on historical stability and capability data.

Example Direct Artifacts
Candidate and selected subprocesses
Historical data used in selection process
Example Indirect Artifacts
Risk evaluation based on selected subprocesses
Review of defined process
Approval of defined process

QPM SP 1.3-1   Select the subprocesses of the project's defined process that
will be statistically managed.

Example Direct Artifacts
Subprocesses that will be statistically managed
Measurement data that will be used to statistically manage the
subprocesses
Example Indirect Artifacts
Measurement data
Statistical analysis results

QPM SP 1.4-1   Monitor the project to determine whether the project's objectives for quality and process performance will be satisfied, and identify corrective action as appropriate.

Example Direct Artifacts
Estimates of probability of meeting objectives
Status reports
Example Indirect Artifacts
Minutes of status report reviews
Statistical analysis results

QPM SG 2   The performance of selected subprocesses within the project's
defined process is statistically managed.

QPM SP 2.1-1   Select the measures and analytic techniques to be used in statistically managing the selected subprocesses.

Example Direct Artifacts
Measure definitions
Measures selected for analysis
Statistical analysis results
Example Indirect Artifacts
Statistical analysis meeting minutes
Senior management review materials of statistical data
Senior management review meeting minutes

QPM SP 2.2-1   Establish and maintain an understanding of the variation of the selected subprocesses using the selected measures and analytic techniques.

Example Direct Artifacts
Process performance analysis results
Statistical process control charts
Example Indirect Artifacts
Minutes of process control meetings
Measurement data
Senior management review materials of statistical data
Senior management review meeting minutes

QPM SP 2.3-1   Monitor the performance of the selected subprocesses to determine their capability to satisfy their quality and process-performance objectives, and identify corrective action as necessary.

Example Direct Artifacts
Statistical process control charts for each selected subprocess
Corrective actions resulting from statistical process control
Example Indirect Artifacts
Status charts
Status review meeting minutes

QPM SP 2.4-1   Record statistical and quality management data in the organization's measurement repository.

Example Direct Artifacts
Measurement repository with measures
Example Indirect Artifacts
Status charts
Status review meeting minutes

Requirements Development (RD) Process Area

RD SG 1   Stakeholder needs, expectations, constraints, and interfaces are collected and translated into customer requirements.

RD SP 1.1-1   Identify and collect stakeholder needs, expectations, constraints, and interfaces for all phases of the product life cycle.

Example Direct Artifacts
> Artifacts indicating stakeholder needs, expectations, and constraints
> that address the various product life-cycle activities have been
> consolidated and conflicts between major stakeholders have been
> resolved to produce the "customer" requirements

Example Indirect Artifacts
> Notes that indicate the stakeholders have agreed to the resolution of
> "conflicts" that surfaced during the gathering and consolidation of their
> needs, expectations, constraints, and possible operational concepts

RD SP 1.1-2   Elicit stakeholder needs, expectations, constraints, and interfaces for all phases of the product's life cycle.

Example Direct Artifacts
> Artifacts indicating stakeholder needs, expectations, and constraints
> that address the various product life-cycle activities have been
> consolidated and conflicts between major stakeholders have been
> resolved to produce the "customer" requirements (implicit and explicit)

Example Indirect Artifacts
> Results of requirements collection methods (such as interviews,
> prototypes, operational scenarios, market surveys, use cases, product
> domain analysis, and reverse engineering)
>
> Notes that indicate the stakeholders have agreed to the resolution of
> "conflicts" that surfaced during the gathering and consolidation of their
> needs, expectations, constraints, and possible operational concepts

RD SP 1.2-1   Transform stakeholder needs, expectations, constraints, and interfaces into customer requirements.

Example Direct Artifacts
> Customer requirements

Example Indirect Artifacts
> Minutes of customer requirements reviews
> Approved requirements
> Interface definitions
> Constraints

RD SG 2   Customer requirements are refined and elaborated to develop product and product-component requirements.

RD SP 2.1-1   Establish and maintain product and product-component requirements, which are based on the customer requirements.

Example Direct Artifacts
> Derived requirements
> Product requirements
> Product component requirements

Example Indirect Artifacts
> Minutes of stakeholder reviews
> Analysis and rationale of cost performance tradeoffs of requirements
> and of life-cycle phases considering business objectives
> Performance modeling results

Description and results of methods (such as house of quality) used to translate customer needs into technical parameters
Requirements traceability matrix

RD SP 2.2-1   Allocate the requirements for each product component.

Example Direct Artifacts
Requirement allocation sheets
Provisional requirement allocations
Derived requirements
Example Indirect Artifacts
Stakeholder review minutes of requirements allocation
Indication of allocated requirements traceability

RD SP 2.3-1   Identify interface requirements.

Example Direct Artifacts
Interface requirements, both external and internal to the product
Interfaces with product-related life-cycle processes such as test
equipment, support systems, and manufacturing facilities
Example Indirect Artifacts
Stakeholder review minutes of interface requirements
Architecture definition
Integration test plans
Configuration management ID for interface descriptions

RD SG 3   The requirements are analyzed and validated, and a definition of required functionality is developed.

RD SP 3.1-1   Establish and maintain operational concepts and associated scenarios.

Example Direct Artifacts
Operational concept
Use cases
Timeline scenarios
Example Indirect Artifacts
Stakeholder review minutes of operational concept
Lower-level detailed requirements
Revision histories
Conceptual solutions
Definition of environment the product will operate in

RD SP 3.2-1   Establish and maintain a definition of required functionality.

Example Direct Artifacts
Functional architecture
Definition of functions
Logical groupings
Association with requirements
Example Indirect Artifacts
Activity diagrams and use cases
Object-oriented analysis with services identified

Results of analysis of requirements for subfunctions that identify logical
or functional partitions of requirements
Definitions of time-critical functions
Traceability of functional requirements that relate to product operation

RD SP 3.3-1   Analyze requirements to ensure that they are necessary and
sufficient.

Example Direct Artifacts
Requirements analysis reports
Requirements traceability matrix or equivalent that shows the path from
the lower-level derived requirements to their higher-level parent
requirements
Example Indirect Artifacts
Proposed requirements changes to resolve defects
Key requirements that are documented and tracked because they have a
strong influence on cost, schedule, functionality, risk, or performance

RD SP 3.4-3   Analyze requirements to balance stakeholder needs and
constraints.

Example Direct Artifacts
Results of requirements analysis indicating impact on cost, schedule,
performance, functionality, reusable components, quality factors such as
maintainability and expandability, or risk
Assessment of risks related to requirements
Example Indirect Artifacts
Action items relating to requirements balancing
Risk mitigation plan

RD SP 3.5-1   Validate requirements to ensure the resulting product will perform appropriately in its intended use environment.

Example Direct Artifacts
Results of requirements validation
Example Indirect Artifacts
Requirements traceability matrix
Requirements changes
Requirements specification

RD SP 3.5-2   Validate requirements to ensure the resulting product will perform as intended in the user's environment using multiple techniques as
appropriate.

Example Direct Artifacts
Results of techniques to demonstrate requirements functionality (such
as prototypes, simulations, analyses, scenarios, and storyboards)
Record of analysis methods and results
Example Indirect Artifacts
Requirements changes
Requirements traceability matrix
Requirements specification
Rationale of why a certain validation technique was used over other
possible techniques and the interpretation of its effectiveness

Requirements Management (REQM) PA

REQM SG 1   Requirements are managed and inconsistencies with project plans and work products are identified.

REQM SP 1.1-1   Develop an understanding with the requirements providers on the meaning of the requirements.

> *Example Direct Artifacts*
>> An agreed-to set of product and/or product component requirements
>> Requirements documents in a mutually acceptably form and format (text, objects, data-flow diagrams, and so on)
>
> *Example Indirect Artifacts*
>> Results of analyses against requirements criteria
>> Evidence of clarification reviews with requirements providers (such as analysis reports, minutes, clarifications, review logs, and requirements updates) resulting in identified requirements issue
>> Action items issued to track resolution of requirements issues
>> Agreement of the requirement by the requirements providers

REQM SP 1.2-2   Obtain commitment to the requirements from the project participants.

> *Example Direct Artifacts*
>> Documented commitments to requirements and requirements changes
>
> *Example Indirect Artifacts*
>> Requirements database reports, with attributes for review / commitment status
>> Requirements change request logs, with recorded commitment
>> Requirements impact assessments
>> Evidence of internal requirements reviews being held (such as minutes, checklists, logs, metrics, and so on) by key members of the project team (such as design authority and team leaders)
>> Communication of requirements to project stakeholders, and involvement in establishing commitment

REQM SP 1.3-1   Manage changes to the requirements as they evolve during the project.

> *Example Direct Artifacts*
>> Requirements change request logs, with recorded commitment (such as signature) and estimates of impact
>> Updated requirements change history with the rationale for the changes
>> Impact analysis for any requirements change request that includes input from all relevant stakeholders
>
> *Example Indirect Artifacts*
>> Requirements status
>> Requirements database
>> Requirements decision database
>> Requirements reports with attributes indicating current state (such as approval, source, rationale, revision history, and impact)
>> Change requests, notices, or proposals

Version control of baselined and documented requirements revisions
Evidence of requirements change reviews during which requirements changes are evaluated with relevant stakeholders, including impact assessment
Revisions to work products resulting from changed requirements

REQM SP 1.4-2   Maintain bi-directional traceability among the requirements and the project plans and work products.

Example Direct Artifacts
Requirements traceability matrix
Reports or database indicating traceability of requirements to/from project plans and work products, at each applicable level of system decomposition
Example Indirect Artifacts
Requirements tracking system
Criteria and completed checklists and minutes for review of requirements traceability
Requirements tracking logs
Revision and maintenance of requirements traceability across the life cycle
Listings of allocated requirements included in reviews of project plans and work products across the life cycle
Requirements mappings used to support impact assessments

REQM SP 1.5-1   Identify inconsistencies between the project plans and work products and the requirements.

Example Direct Artifacts
Documentation of identified requirements inconsistencies including sources, conditions, and rationales
Corrective actions
Example Indirect Artifacts
Completed checklists, forms, logs, action items, or minutes substantiating reviews of requirements consistency with the project plans, activities, or work products

Risk Management (RSKM) PA

RSKM SG 1   Preparation for risk management is conducted.

RSKM SP 1.1-1   Determine risk sources and categories.

Example Direct Artifacts
Risk sources lists (external and internal)
Risk categories list
Example Indirect Artifacts
Risk taxonomy or hierarchy (such as risk classes, elements, and attributes)
Risk management tool or database

RSKM SP 1.2-1   Define the parameters used to analyze and categorize risks, and the parameters used to control the risk management effort.

Example Direct Artifacts
 Risk evaluation, categorization, and prioritization criteria
 Risk management requirements (control and approval levels,
 reassessment intervals, and so on)
Example Indirect Artifacts
 Risk management tool or database
 Defined ranges and parameters for risk evaluation, categorization, and
 prioritization, such as risk likelihood (probability) and consequence
 (severity)
 Defined thresholds (such as control points, scoping boundary
 conditions, exclusions, and triggers) and criteria for taking action

RSKM SP 1.3-1 Establish and maintain the strategy to be used for risk management.

Example Direct Artifacts
 Project risk management strategy
 Risk management plan
Example Indirect Artifacts
 Evidence of reviews of the risk management strategy held with project
 stakeholders (such as signature approval, minutes, and action items)
 Measures identified for monitoring risk status
 Risk management procedures and tools
 Description and application of risk mitigation techniques (prototyping,
 simulation, and so on)

RSKM SG 2 Risks are identified and analyzed to determine their relative importance.

RSKM SP 2.1-1 Identify and document the risks.

Example Direct Artifacts
 List of identified risks, including the context, conditions, and
 consequences for occurrence
 Revisions to list of identified risks
Example Indirect Artifacts
 Structured risk statements
 Risk assessment results or evidence of occurrence
 Risk taxonomy-based questionnaire interviews

RSKM SP 2.2-1 Evaluate and categorize each identified risk using the defined risk categories and parameters, and determine its relative priority.

Example Direct Artifacts
 List of risks, with a priority assigned to each risk
 Categorization and parameter values of identified risks
Example Indirect Artifacts
 Project reviews or briefings of risks and risk parameters
 Aggregated and consolidated set of risks, with cause and effect
 relationships identified between related risks
 Derived measures for identified risks (such as risk exposure)

RSKM SG 3   Risks are handled and mitigated, where appropriate, to reduce adverse impacts on achieving objectives.

RSKM SP 3.1-1   Develop a risk mitigation plan for the most important risks to the project, as defined by the risk management strategy.

> *Example Direct Artifacts*
>> Risk mitigation plans
>> Contingency plans
> *Example Indirect Artifacts*
>> List of those responsible for tracking and addressing each risk
>> Documented handling options for each identified risk
>> Risk levels and thresholds defined to trigger deployment of risk mitigation plans
>> Management reserve budget allocation for deployment of risk mitigation plans

RSKM SP 3.2-1   Monitor the status of each risk periodically and implement the risk mitigation plan as appropriate.

> *Example Direct Artifacts*
>> Updated lists of risk status
>> Updated assessments of risk likelihood, consequence, and thresholds
>> Implemented risk mitigation actions or contingency plans
> *Example Indirect Artifacts*
>> Evidence of risk management status reviews (periodic and event-driven)
>> Risk status reports, analyses, performance measures, and trending
>> Updated lists of risk-handling options
>> Updated list of actions taken to handle risks
>> Risk mitigation plans
>> Newly identified risks
>> Risk-handling actions, tracked to closure

Supplier Agreement Management (SAM) PA

SAM SG 1   Agreements with suppliers are established and maintained.

SAM SP 1.1-1   Determine the type of acquisition for each product or product component to be acquired.

> *Example Direct Artifacts*
>> List of the acquisition types that will be used for all products and product components to be acquired
> *Example Indirect Artifacts*
>> Make/buy analysis or trade study with product acquisition options
>> Management authorization to proceed with acquisition of a product or service
>> System architecture/design documentation identifying products or components to be acquired (such as non-developmental items)

SAM SP 1.2-1   Select suppliers based on an evaluation of their ability to meet the specified requirements and established criteria.

Example Direct Artifacts
Rationale for selection of suppliers
Evaluation criteria
Supplier evaluation results
Example Indirect Artifacts
Source selection decision
List of candidate suppliers
Preferred supplier list
Advantages and disadvantages of candidate suppliers
Solicitation materials and requirements
Requirements allocation to the product to be acquired
Procurement documentation (such as tech spec, SOW, interfaces, solicitation, proposals, and so on)
Supplier surveys
Analysis of acquisition risks and best value supplier

SAM SP 1.3-1   Establish and maintain formal agreements with the supplier.

Example Direct Artifacts
Documented formal supplier agreement, with approved revisions as necessary
Statements of work
Contracts
Memoranda of agreement
Licensing agreement
Example Indirect Artifacts
Negotiated contractual terms, conditions, and constraints (e.g., deliverables, requirements, schedule, budget, standards, facilities, and acceptance criteria)
Defined parameters, criteria, and objectives for evaluating supplier performance
Acquirer impact assessment and revision to project plans, as necessary
Supplier work breakdown structure
Issues or action items relating to definition or revision of the supplier agreement

SAM SG 2   Agreements with the suppliers are satisfied by both the project and the supplier.

SAM SP 2.1-1   Review candidate COTS products to satisfy the specified requirements that are covered under a supplier agreement.

Example Direct Artifacts
Reviews of COTS products
Identification of selected COTS products with rationale for selection
Example Indirect Artifacts
Trade studies
Supplier performance reports

Negotiated licenses or agreements for purchase of COTS products
Requirements allocation to COTS products or components
Checklists, criteria, risk assessments, or trade studies for evaluation and selection of COTS products

SAM SP 2.2-1   Perform activities with the supplier as specified in the supplier agreement.

Example Direct Artifacts
Supplier progress reports and performance measures
Supplier review materials and report
Documentation of work product and document deliveries
Example Indirect Artifacts
Action items tracked to closure
Audits, corrective action requests, and plans to improve supplier performance
Supporting evidence of supplier technical and management reviews (agenda, minutes, and so on)

SAM SP 2.3-1   Ensure that the supplier agreement is satisfied before accepting the acquired product.

Example Direct Artifacts
Acceptance test results
Configuration audit results
Verification of functional performance, configuration, and adherence to defined requirements and commitments
Example Indirect Artifacts
Acceptance test procedures
Discrepancy reports or corrective action plans
Traceability reports indicating coverage of requirements for the acquired product by acceptance test procedures
Closure or termination of supplier agreement

SAM SP 2.4-1   Transition the acquired products from the supplier to the project.

Example Direct Artifacts
Transition plans
Records reflecting implementation of transition plans
Example Indirect Artifacts
Training reports
Support and maintenance reports
CM reports indicating control, auditing, and maintenance of acquired products
Records indicating integration of the acquired product into the project
Vendor maintenance agreements

Technical Solution (TS) Process Area

TS SG 1   Product or product-component solutions are selected from alternative solutions.

TS SP 1.1-1   Develop alternative solutions and establish selection criteria.

> *Example Direct Artifacts*
>> Alternative solutions
>> Selection criteria
>
> *Example Indirect Artifacts*
>> Evaluation of solutions and technologies (new or legacy)
>> Requirements allocation for each alternative and their associated cost
>> Design issues
>> A process or processes for identifying solution alternatives, selection criteria, and design issues
>> COTS evaluations

TS SP 1.1-2   Develop detailed alternative solutions and selection criteria.

> *Example Direct Artifacts*
>> Alternative solutions that span the acceptable range of cost, schedule, performance, and quality
>> Evaluations of new technologies
>> Selection criteria for final selection, which may include
>>> Technical performance
>>> Complexity of the product component
>>> Product expansion and growth
>>> Sensitivity to construction methods and materials
>>> Capabilities and limitations of end users
>
> *Example Indirect Artifacts*
>> Review minutes of alternative solutions

TS SP 1.2-2   Evolve the operational concept, scenarios, and environments to describe the conditions, operating modes, and operating states specific to each product component.

> *Example Direct Artifacts*
>> Product component operational concepts, scenarios, and environments for all pertinent life-cycle processes (operations, support, training, manufacturing, verification, deployment/fielding/delivery/disposal)
>
> *Example Indirect Artifacts*
>> Review minutes of the operational concept
>> Timeline analyses of product component interactions
>> Use cases for each product component
>> Criteria and checklists used for describing the conditions, operating modes, and operating states of each component
>> Change requests

TS SP 1.3-1   Select the product component solutions that best satisfy the criteria established.

Example Direct Artifacts
> Product component selection decisions and rationale
> Documented relationships between requirements and product components
> Documentation of selected solutions using the allocated requirements and selected product components

Example Indirect Artifacts
> Review minutes of the selection
> Resolution of issues for selection of best alternative solution using the functional requirements as a parameter

TS SG 2   Product or product-component designs are developed.

TS SP 2.1-1   Develop a design for the product or product component.

Example Direct Artifacts
> Product architecture
> Product capabilities
>> Product partitions
>> Product-component identifications
>> Systems states
>> Major intercomponent interfaces
>> External product interfaces
> Product component detailed designs
> Fully characterized interfaces

Example Indirect Artifacts
> Minutes of design reviews
> Structural elements
> Updated traceability matrix

TS SP 2.2-1   Establish and maintain a technical data package.

Example Direct Artifacts
> Technical data package
>> Drawings
>> Specifications
>> Design descriptions
>> Design databases
>> Performance requirements
>> Quality assurance provisions
>> Packaging details
>> Different views that were captured to help organize data defining design descriptions

Example Indirect Artifacts
> Technical data package review minutes

TS SP 2.3-1   Establish and maintain the solution for product component interfaces.

Example Direct Artifacts
> Interface design
> Interface design documents

Revision history and descriptions of changes incorporated to controlled interfaces.

Example Indirect Artifacts

Interface requirements, internal and external to the product

Interfaces between product components and the product-related life cycles

Interface control and design documents

Interface specification criteria, templates, and checklists used by design team

TS SP 2.3-3   Design comprehensive product component interfaces in terms of established and maintained criteria.

Example Direct Artifacts

Interface design specifications

    Origination

    Destination

    Stimulus and data characteristics for software

    Electrical, mechanical, and functional characteristics of the hardware

Interface control documents

Rationale for selected interface design

Revision history and descriptions of changes incorporated to controlled interfaces

Example Indirect Artifacts

Interface review minutes

Interface requirements—internal and external to the product

Interface control and design documents

Interface specification criteria, templates, and checklists (see model for typical parameters and characteristics that are investigated)

TS SP 2.4-3   Evaluate whether the product components should be developed, purchased, or reused based on established criteria.

Example Direct Artifacts

Criteria for design and component reuse

Make or buy analyses including the factors that were taken into consideration

    Functions the products or services will provide

    Available project resources and skills

    Costs of acquiring versus developing internally

    Strategic business alliances

    Market research of available products

    Functionality and quality of available products

    Skills and capabilities of potential suppliers

    Product availability

Example Indirect Artifacts

Guidance for choosing COTS components

    Supplier agreements

    Reuse component libraries, guidance, and criteria for reuse of *non-developmental items* (NDI)

Evaluation criteria, rationale, and reports for make-buy analyses and product component selection
Plans for maintenance, support, and transition of COTS/NDI components
Product acceptance criteria
Product operational, maintenance, and support concepts

TS SG 3   Product components, and associated support documentation, are implemented from their designs.

TS SP 3.1-1   Implement the designs of the product components.

Example Direct Artifacts
Implemented design
Product component implementation and support data (such as source code, documented data and services, fabricated parts, deployed manufacturing processes, facilities, and materials)
Example Indirect Artifacts
Results of peer reviews, inspections, or verifications performed on constructed components
Unit test plans, procedures, results, and acceptance criteria
Configuration and change control data for revision to product components

TS SP 3.2-1   Develop and maintain the end-use documentation.

Example Direct Artifacts
End-user training materials
User's manual
Operator's manual
Maintenance manual
Installation manual
Example Indirect Artifacts
Artifacts related to peer review of applicable documentation
Site installation, training, and maintenance records

Validation (PP) PA

VAL SG 1   Preparation for validation is conducted.

VAL SP 1.1-1   Select products and product components to be validated and the validation methods that will be used for each.

Example Direct Artifacts
Lists of products and product components selected for validation
Validation methods for each product or product component
Example Indirect Artifacts
Requirements for performing validation for each product or product component
Validation constraints for each product or product component
Evaluation criteria defined
Stakeholder reviews of validation methods
Validation plans and procedures

VAL SP 1.2-2   Establish and maintain the environment needed to support validation.

Example Direct Artifacts
　　Validation environment
Example Indirect Artifacts
　　Resource plan, including reuse of existing resources
　　Review minutes of validation environment

VAL SP 1.3-3   Establish and maintain procedures and criteria for validation.

Example Direct Artifacts
　　Validation procedures
　　Validation criteria
Example Indirect Artifacts
　　Reviews of validation procedures and criteria
　　Test and evaluation procedures for maintenance, training, and support
　　Product requirements mapping to validation procedures and methods

VAL SG 2   The product or product components are validated to ensure that they are suitable for use in their intended operating environment.

VAL SP 2.1-1   Perform validation on the selected products and product components.

Example Direct Artifacts
　　Validation reports
　　Validation results
　　As-run procedures log
Example Indirect Artifacts
　　Data collected from performing validation procedures
　　Validation cross-reference matrix
　　Operational demonstrations
　　List of deviations encountered during execution of validation
　　procedures

VAL SP 2.2-1   Capture and analyze the results of the validation activities and identify issues.

Example Direct Artifacts
　　Validation deficiency reports
　　Validation issues
　　Analysis reports
　　Validation results
Example Indirect Artifacts
　　Minutes of reviews of validation results
　　Procedure change request
　　Validation evaluation criteria
　　Comparison of actual versus expected results (such as measurements
　　and performance data)

Verification (VER) PA

VER SG 1   Preparation for verification is conducted.

VER SP 1.1-1   Select the work products to be verified and the verification methods that will be used for each.

Example Direct Artifacts
    Lists of work products selected for verification
    Verification methods for each selected work product
Example Indirect Artifacts
    Peer review plans
    Requirements verification matrix with traceability to work products
    Verification cross-reference matrix
    Verification plan
    Reverification approach (such as regression testing)

VER SP 1.2-2   Establish and maintain the environment needed to support verification.

Example Direct Artifacts
    Verification environment
Example Indirect Artifacts
    Requirements for the verification environment
    Definition of verification support equipment and tools
    Acquisition plan for verification environment components (such as COTS, reuse of existing assets, and custom developed tools)
    Plans or reports tracking availability of verification environment components

VER SP 1.3-3   Establish and maintain verification procedures and criteria for the selected work products.

Example Direct Artifacts
    Verification procedures
    Verification criteria
Example Indirect Artifacts
    Expected results and tolerances identified
    Equipment and environmental components identified

VER SG 2   Peer reviews are performed on selected work products.

VER SP 2.1-1   Prepare for peer reviews of selected work products.

Example Direct Artifacts
    Peer review data package
    Peer review schedule
    Selected work products to be reviewed
    Peer review plans, processes, and schedules
Example Indirect Artifacts
    Peer review checklist
    Entry and exit criteria for work products

Criteria for requiring another peer review
Peer review training material
Description of method chosen for the peer review, such as inspections, walkthroughs, and so on
Peer review preparation metrics

VER SP 2.2-1   Conduct peer reviews on selected work products to identify issues resulting from the peer reviews.

Example Direct Artifacts
Peer review results
Peer review issues
Peer review data
Identified defects
Data summarizing the conduct and results of the peer review
Example Indirect Artifacts
Schedules showing peer reviews and re-review
Action items for corrective action
Peer review data repository
Completed peer review checklists

VER SP 2.3-2   Analyze data about preparation, conduct, and results of the peer reviews.

Example Direct Artifacts
Peer review data
Data recorded to reflect the conduct of the review (preparation, conduct, and results)
Documented peer review analysis results
Example Indirect Artifacts
Peer review action items
Peer review data repository
List of action items produced during peer reviews

VER SG 3   Selected work products are verified against their specified requirements.

VER SP 3.1-1   Perform verification on the selected work products.

Example Direct Artifacts
Verification results
Test results
Peer review results
Verification reports
As-run procedures log
Example Indirect Artifacts
Demonstrations
Action items identified

VER SP 3.2-2   Analyze the results of all verification activities and identify corrective action.

Example Direct Artifacts
   Analysis report (such as statistics on performances, causal analysis of
   non-conformances, comparison of the behavior between the real
   product and models, and trends)
   Corrective actions to verification methods, criteria, and/or
   infrastructure
   Corrective actions identified for verified products
Example Indirect Artifacts
   Trouble reports
   Method, criteria, and infrastructure change requests

Capability Level 2

GG 2   The process is institutionalized as a managed process.

GP 2.1   Establish and maintain an organizational policy for planning and performing the process.

Example Direct Artifacts
   Organizational policy
Example Indirect Artifacts
   Policy repository

GP 2.2   Establish and maintain the plan for performing the process.

Example Direct Artifacts
   Project plan (identify location of specific plans relative to PA)
Example Indirect Artifacts
   Approval of plan
   Peer review of plan

GP 2.3   Provide adequate resources for performing the process, developing
the work products, and providing the services of the process.

Example Direct Artifacts
   Budget
   Schedule
   People
   Facilities
Example Indirect Artifacts
   Actuals of budget, staffing, facilities

GP 2.4   Assign responsibility and authority for performing the process,
developing the work products, and providing the services of the process.

Example Direct Artifacts
   Organization chart
   Charter
   Responsibilities, Authority, Consult, Inform matrix
Example Indirect Artifacts
   Actual labor charges
   Approvals of work products

GP 2.5   Train the people performing or supporting the process as needed.

Example Direct Artifacts
   Training records
Example Indirect Artifacts
   Training model for roles

GP 2.6   Place designated work products of the process under appropriate levels of configuration management.

Example Direct Artifacts
   Work products under CM
Example Indirect Artifacts
   Release documents
   CCB minutes

GP 2.7   Identify and involve the relevant stakeholders as planned.

Example Direct Artifacts
   Stakeholder meeting minutes
   Technical interchange meeting minutes
   Stakeholder matrix showing roles
Example Indirect Artifacts
   Signatures on documents
   Action items assigned to stakeholders

GP 2.8   Monitor and control the process against the plan for performing the process and take appropriate corrective action.

Example Direct Artifacts
   Weekly status meeting minutes
   Measurement analysis meeting minutes
Example Indirect Artifacts
   Action items from weekly status meetings
   Action items from measurement analysis meetings
   Management review minutes reporting monitor and control activities

GP 2.9   Objectively evaluate adherence of the process against its process description, standards, and procedures, and address noncompliance.

Example Direct Artifacts
   Audit reports
   Objective review meeting minutes
   Noncompliance records
Example Indirect Artifacts
   Audit checklists
   Objective review materials
   Management review minutes reporting audit results
   Noncompliance status reports

GP 2.10   Review the activities, status, and results of the process with higher-level management and resolve issues.

Example Direct Artifacts
    Senior management review materials
    Action items from senior management reviews
Example Indirect Artifacts
    Senior management review meeting minutes
    Action item status from senior management reviews

Capability Level 3

GG 3   The process is institutionalized as a defined process.

GP 3.1   Establish and maintain the description of a defined process.

Example Direct Artifacts
    Tailoring work products
Example Indirect Artifacts
    Approval of tailoring

GP 3.2   Collect work products, measures, measurement results, and improvement information derived from planning and performing the process to support the future use and improvement of the organization's processes and process assets.

Example Direct Artifacts
    Measures collected in organizational measurement repository
    Lessons learned in process asset library
    Work products in process asset library
    Measurement analysis results in process asset library
Example Indirect Artifacts
    Process asset library metrics or records
    Organizational reports of measurement repository

SEI Figure Credit List

Index

U-Z

Register Your Book

at www.awprofessional.com/register

You may be eligible to receive:

- Advance notice of forthcoming editions of the book
- Related book recommendations
- Chapter excerpts and supplements of forthcoming titles
- Information about special contests and promotions throughout the year
- Notices and reminders about author appearances, tradeshows, and online chats with special guests

Contact us

If you are interested in writing a book or reviewing manuscripts prior to publication, please write to us at:

Editorial Department
Addison-Wesley Professional
75 Arlington Street, Suite 300
Boston, MA 02116 USA
Email: AWPro@aw.com

Addison-Wesley

Visit us on the Web: http://www.awprofessional.com

The SEI Series in Software Engineering

ISBN 0-321-18613-3

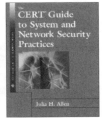

ISBN 0-321-11886-3

ISBN 0-201-73723-X

ISBN 0-321-15495-9

ISBN 0-201-54664-7

ISBN 0-321-15496-7

ISBN 0-201-70372-6

ISBN 0-201-70482-X

ISBN 0-201-70332-7

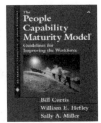

ISBN 0-201-60445-0

ISBN 0-201-60444-2

ISBN 0-201-52577-1

ISBN 0-201-25592-8

ISBN 0-201-54597-7

ISBN 0-201-54809-7

ISBN 0-201-18095-2

ISBN 0-201-54610-8

ISBN 0-201-47719-X

ISBN 0-201-77639-1

ISBN 0-201-61626-2

ISBN 0-201-70454-4

ISBN 0-201-73409-5

ISBN 0-201-85480-5

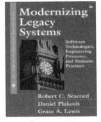

ISBN 0-321-11884-7

ISBN 0-201-70064-6

Please see our Web site at http://www.awprofessional.com for more information on these titles.